A Unique
African
American
Approach to
Stewardship

From Proclamation to Practice

A Unique
African
American
Approach to
Stewardship

From Proclamation to Practice

Clifford A. Jones Sr., *Editor*

Judson Press ® Valley Forge

Library of Congress Cataloging-in-Publication Data

From proclamation to practice : a unique African American approach to
  stewardship / Clifford A. Jones, editor.
     p. cm.
     Includes bibliographical references.
     ISBN 0-8170-1192-7
     1. Stewardship, Christian. 2. Afro-American—Religion.
I. Jones, Clifford A.
BV772.F68 1993
248'.6'08996073-dc20

93-10314

Dedicated to all African American preachers of the gospel
of our Lord Jesus Christ,
and especially to the memory of:

**The Reverend James Pedew, who saw the call of God upon me
before I heard his voice.**

**The Reverend Murphy "Pop" Grier
of the Aenon Baptist Church in Rochester, New York,
who licensed me to preach.**

**The Reverend Doctor Homer B. Fergurson,
my pastor who ordained me to preach
through the Mud Creek Association in Asheville, North Carolina.**

All of whom have gone home.

Table of Contents

Foreword

Stewardship is what a person does with his or her life after saying, "I believe!"

There is no experience in the African American church as vital to its history as stewardship. Stewardship in many expressions has often been the unheralded paradigm for the amazing success story of the church in its total witness to the African American community.

The preaching and teaching and usage of the language of stewardship has been a key component of the African American church experience.

Growing up in Ebenezer Baptist Church in segregated Atlanta, Georgia, in the 1940s, we children were taught to always "remember the Lord" with our money, our time, and our talents. We were to give at every worship service or church family gathering. There was always an offering. No matter how poor we might have been, we were all able to give, even if it was just a penny out of a dime. Tithing was the way to give thanks to God by giving back to God that which was already God's. This was the general experience that prevailed and still prevails in the African American churches.

From Proclamation to Practice: A Unique African American Approach to Stewardship is a compilation of the preaching, teaching, practice, and biblical foundations of Christian stewardship in the African American churches. Dr. Clifford A. Jones, Sr., has assembled an outstanding cadre of African American clergy, each of whom shares in the presentation of the preaching and practice of biblical stewardship.

This work is a chronicle of the history of thought in African American stewardship practices as well as a blueprint for the continuous development and practice of stewardship as a pattern of commitment for the future. It is unique in that it brings together the African American stewardship experience from many voices, giving affirmation to the sacred place of stewardship in the African American idiom.

This book celebrates the "new creation" that sees one's life as a total stewardship stage upon which is acted out the gratitude of a humble steward to a generous God. In vivid clarity, it presents stewardship as a way of living.

The African American church preaches and teaches stewardship as a total way of life. Its preachers develop the climate for a true cultivation of all the riches of God's gifts to us as stewards, thereby opening the door to greater gifts in the fulfillment of the church's mission to "proclaim the good news."

The message is strong: If any man or woman be in Christ, he or she is a new being—one who recognizes and acknowledges his or her stewardship of life before God.

> Take my life and let it be
> consecrated, Lord, to thee. . . .
> Take my hands, and let them move
> At the impulse of thy love.
>
> Take my silver and my gold
> Not a mite would I withhold.
> Take my moments and my days
> Let them flow in ceaseless praise.[1]

This is the message of the Christian steward. This is the message of this book. This is the spirit of African American stewardship.

Dr. Albert Paul Brinson
Associate Director, World Mission Support
Office of the General Secretary
American Baptist Churches in the U.S.A.

Preface

Preaching occurs in the traditional context of worship. During the preaching moment, the essential objective of the preacher, whose assignment and calling is divine, is to elevate the Word of God among the people of God, creating an atmosphere for nurture, affirmation, repentance, hope, and renewed commitment to God through a faith response in the name of Jesus the Christ. Capturing the divine-human relationship of the Caller and called, the Sender and sent during the preaching moment is like holding the twilight, or seeing the interplay of ethereal currents, or touching the essence of natural love. The preacher approaches the "Sacred Desk" with emotions of tension and tears, anxiety and anticipation, fear of failure and hope for a powerful, informed anointing of the Spirit. This is why the true pulpit . . .

> Must stand acknowledged while the world shall stand,
> The most important and effectual guard,
> Support, and ornament of Virtue's cause
> There stands the messenger of truth: there stands
> The legate of the skies—His theme divine,
> His office sacred, his Credentials clear.
> By him the violated law speaks out
> Its thunders; and by him, in strains as sweet
> As angels use, the Gospel whispers peace.
> William Cowper, *The Task, Book II*

This book is developed from the African American Christian perspective. The contributors are ministers who have given their attention to the development of historical patterns and trends shaping the Christian religious experience of African Americans. These are patterns, trends, and customs that cannot be ignored in developing vital ministries through stewardship in the twenty-first century. Through diversified ministries these preachers have demonstrated a keen awareness of critical issues that confront and will confront the African American Christian church. The challenge is to affirm traditional African American stewardship—giving patterns—and acknowledge the present indicative of biblical stewardship through tithing as a *fait accompli*. Consequently, we have the title *From Proclamation to Practice: A Unique African American Approach to Stewardship*. The uniqueness of this work is that it affirms the centrality of preaching and its influence on all aspects of the church's ministry. If the reverend will say it, and stick to it, others will follow. The biblical principle of tithing must be proclaimed if it is to be practiced.

While in revival a minister was spiritually led to speak about the necessity of practical stewardship through tithing, at which time hands stopped waving, the hallelujahs ceased, and an eerie silence filled that place. After the benediction a gentleman came forward, shook the minister's hand, and, looking him sharply in the eye, said, "You let us off too easy on tithing tonight. Tell 'em, Rev, that they got to tithe. I just now learned what it meant, and since I started, the Lord's been blessing me. You let us off easy; we need to hear the message of tithing. Keep on preaching!"

Probably the major obstacle that confronts the preaching and practice of biblical stewardship is the assumption that it is all about money, money, and more money. Although money is involved in one's stewardship, it is not an end but a means by which the church can actualize the ministries and mission of Christ. This is ably demonstrated in the sermons that are presented relating to issues that confront the church now and into the twenty-first century. With dwindling political "pork-barrel funds," an emphasis on community involvement, and the overt sentiment that African Americans have had long enough to catch up, it will become more and more of a necessity that African American churches involve themselves in enhancing the cultural, physical, emotional, and spiritual development of its native daughters and sons. It is to this end that this work is presented.

Initial discussion for this book and other related materials about stewardship from the African American perspective started with a Task Force on Stewardship in Black Congregations through the World Mission Support office of the American Baptist Churches in the U.S.A., initially chaired by the Reverend Allen Paul Weaver in 1985. As a result of its efforts, a "Planning Manual for Call to Commitment" was produced through permission of the World Mission Support office. The task force members—William Thurmond, Chair; Alfloyd Butler; Jacob Chatman; Lee Jefferson; Clifford A. Jones, Sr.; Arthur Manning; Earl Miller; Milton Owens, Jr.; O. T. Tomes—and staff supporters—O. John Eldred, Richard Rusbuldt, Albert Paul Brinson, James Widmer, Patricia Merchant, Robert Roberts, and Ronald Vallet—gave countless hours and energy, which are reflected in this work. Deep appreciation is expressed to the Friendship Missionary Baptist Church for accepting the challenge to be intentional in ministry through biblical stewardship. The secretarial staff of Phyliss Caldwell, Fannie French, and Sandra Lee worked beyond the call of their job descriptions in writing correspondence and typing parts of this work. Special appreciation is extended to Milton Owens, who demonstrated courage and faith during his personal crisis and is a stalwart in the kingdom of God. Rosa Scarborough used her talent and time in proofreading this entire work and enhancing its quality.

This work would not be, of course, except that these preachers shared their quality time in accepting this challenge to be creative in approaching the topic of stewardship. They are pastors, preachers, evangelists, and teachers of the first magnitude—The Reverends Jason A. Barr, Jr.; Albert Paul Brinson; James A. Forbes, Jr.; Arlee Griffin, Jr.; G. Daniel Jones; William A. Lawson, Jr.; Ella Pearson Mitchell; Robert G. Murray; Milton E. Owens, Jr.; James C. Perkins; S. A. Raper; William J. Shaw; Laura B. Sinclair; J. Alfred Smith, Sr.; O. T. Tomes; Johnny L. White, Sr.; W. D. Woods; and Jeremiah A. Wright, Jr. It is impossible to capture on paper the style, mood, spirit, mannerisms, and verbal power of these preachers. Consequently, in some instances a verbal preaching style took precedence over written literary form.

The preacher's family has additional stress and strain because of the demands of the Divine, church, and community. I am grateful for the patience and love of my wife, Brenda; Michelle, my daughter and friend; Renee, my special daughter; Anthony, Jr., my namesake; and all of my children. Thank you for being who you are and for your prayers and love.

It is customary for the author to share whatever blessings result from a work like this and—hopefully posthumously—accept whatever ills or criticism are forthcoming. However, I relinquish the rights for the criticism to be mutually shared, and pray that through the merits of this work, God may be actualized through Jesus the Christ.

From Proclamation

Preaching Stewardship: The Word of God

Clifford A. Jones, Sr.

The reverend made an earnest and compassionate appeal for the congregation to "really give" during the mission offering because of the escalating demands in the community and foreign field. During the joint board meeting of deacons and trustees, the Monday after the fourth Sunday, several complained about the reverend talking so much about money. A penurious yet pompous trustee pointed his finger at the reverend and said, "All this begging and giving will kill the church." It was difficult for the reverend to see this kind of narrow, cold, uninformed attitude among the officers. The leaders of the church, the bearers of Holy Communion each first Sunday, the collectors and counters of the tithes and offerings, the chief stewards and devotional leaders—these are they who have been ordained and affirmed to render leadership in the church, yet their attitude is, "All this begging and giving will kill the church!" The reverend, with obvious pain and disappointment, replied, "Take me to one church that died from giving, and I will leap upon its grave and shout to high heaven, 'Blessed are the dead who die in the Lord henceforth, that they may rest from their labors, for their deeds follow them!' " (see Revelation 14:13).

This chilly atmosphere toward giving and a call for committed stewardship is prevalent. Consequently the reverend is subjugated to scorn, accused of begging, and even has his or her personal and professional integrity questioned. The twenty-first-century African American Christian church would do well to consider a structured, systematic approach to stewardship as a more excellent ministry. If congregations actualized blessings through the stewardship of tithing, there would be no need for fund-raising schemes, parking-lot sales, raffles,

---

Clifford A. Jones, Sr., is senior minister of Friendship Missionary Baptist Church, Charlotte, North Carolina. He currently serves as first vice president of the Lott Carey Foreign Mission Convention and is vice-president-at-large and a former chairman of moderators of the General Baptist State Convention of North Carolina, Inc. He is active in many religious and civic organizations in North Carolina.

bazaars, twelve-tribes rallies, baby contests, fuel drives, and selling plates to financially support the work of Christ through the local church. It may be that some of these activities could provide opportunities for fellowship and service to the community, but their prime function would not be to raise money, and the reverend would not need to plead, urge, and beg to keep things going. A stewardship-ministry-oriented church will not die spiritually or materially. It is only when a church ceases to be Christ-centered and ministry-oriented that it dies.

Reverend, you are essential in nurturing the church and reorientating first leaders and then the entire congregation in principles of biblical stewardship. Dr. W. E. B. DuBois has said:

> The preacher is the most unique personality developed by the Negro on American soil. A leader, a politician, an orator, a "boss," an intriguer, an idealist—all these he is, and ever, too, the center of a group of men, now twenty, and a thousand in number. The combination of a certain adroitness with deep-seated earnestness of tact with consummate ability, gave him the preeminence and helps him maintain it.[1]

These earned attributes enable the reverend to be in the unique position to lead the church to realizing the demands of the eschatological now. Time is of the essence, as the church realizes that its calling is not from the church covenant, or moderator, or auxiliary presidents, but from the Divine. The one called as minister was first of all divinely set apart not to be merely pastor but an instrument of the Divine to lead in actualizing the kingdom of God on earth. Unfortunately, the reverends are allowing significant others to define whose they are: "Chief Executive Officer," "Church Public Relations Specialist," "Chief Administrator," "Word Specialist," "Fund-raising Consultant," and the list goes on. William Henry reported in *Time* magazine on two evangelists of the eighties whose assets evaporated as a result of scandals, saying that "the proceedings will also offer further disputing evidence that leading televangelists saw preaching as a business rather than a calling."[2] The reverend must tenaciously fight the palatable, lucrative lures of packing the sermon with sweets as if nurturing a pasture of unweaned sucklers simply because it is marketable. Incentives are never to be substituted for inspiration.

There is a "gone-wrong-ness" in the body of Christ when cliquish marketing strategies are utilized for the acquisition of fat profits more than for factual prophets. There is a "gone-wrong-ness" in the body of Christ when churches allow only traditions, customs—"the way we have always done it"—and refuse to be led by the Holy Spirit to new creative ministries through biblical stewardship. There is a "gone-wrong-ness" in the body of Christ when the sermon is reduced to a little talk or lecture laden with funny short stories and the preacher relegated to a warm teacher and lecturer who consoles, comforts, and specializes in warm fuzzies while taking only twenty-two minutes during the worship hour.

No sermon is of any value when God does not speak through the preacher. According to Rudolph Bultmann, it is in the New Testament that we learn that "a sermon is an attempt to speak the Word of God to the concrete situation of the hearers so that it may readily be understood."[3] The commission is to "preach the Word" and not allow yourself to become so entangled with this world's goods that the sermon becomes clanging cymbals and sounding brass. A sermon that rambles everywhere hits nothing. The unfocused sermon is like the National Guard playing taps over a fallen comrade. They aim their rifles into the air and shoot their big guns. They make a great big bang, and the nervous family and friends jump. They know it's only a harmless noise, however, because they are shooting blank shells. And the irony is that this ritual is designed for the dead.

The apostles preached as the Holy Spirit gave them utterance. Where the Divine does not give the words, there is no sermon. At best it is vain, vociferant, or rhythmic reading, humming homiletics, or repetitive reciting—profitless preaching. Claude Thompson used to ask his preaching students what would happen if at 10:45 A.M. on Sunday—or even 11:15 A.M.—they suddenly discovered some unrepentant demon had stolen their sermon notes.[4] When the people of God are expecting a fresh word, what do you do when your written notes, the unmemorized poem, the quote that gave authority and credence to the message—all are gone. Professor Thompson suggested that it is in this crisis hour that God says, "For after all, the Gospel is the witness from the innermost soul of the servant of God who has wrestled 'until the break of day' refusing to let God go. If in that hour the man of God bears witness to the Gospel of New Life—because he, too, is alive—he is God's prophet indeed!"[5] When the Divine speaks through the reverend, there are words of consolation and confirmation, words of conviction and conversion, words of judgment and justice, words of suffering and sanctification, words of death and life. When the Divine speaks, the kingdom of God and the redemptive act of Calvary transform nonbelievers from the "was" to the "is" of biblical stewardship. To present the Christian faith obscurely and futuristically is to fail the burning needs of the church. Whenever preaching is degraded into citations of contemporary opinions and human semantic engineering, it betrays the faith committed to the saints. Author James Stewart said:

Let no one listening to your preaching have any doubt that when we Christians say that the dark demonic powers which leave their dreadful trail of devastation across the world are ultimately less powerful than Jesus, we really mean it—just as the early disciples meant it when they declared that Christ had raided the realm of Satan and broken the fast-bound chains of hell.[6]

There is authority in preaching the gospel of the Lord Jesus Christ as participants in the kingdom of God affirming the divine call; therefore the preacher can be bold in proclamation. Emil Brunner said, "Authoritative preaching is the free gift of God. We can never 'possess' the Word of God; we can only pray that it be granted to us when we have to preach."[7] Consequently, preaching is always to be acknowledged as a divine event in spite of the preacher who in reality is inconsequential. H. H. Farmer described preaching as:

> . . . that divine, saying activity in history, which began two thousand years ago in the advent of Christ and in his personal relationship with men and women, and has continued throughout the ages in the sphere of redeemed personal relationship . . . not focusing on me . . . This focusing on me is not apart from what has gone before, nor can it be, for it is part of the continuous purpose throughout the years which began in Christ; hence preaching is telling me something. But it is never merely telling me something. It is God actively probing me, challenging my will, calling on me for decision, offering me his succor.[8]

The story is told of a deacon who slipped a note on the pulpit that said, "Stick to your text—and some of it will stick to us." The preached word is like an envelope—it needs a name, address, and stamp on it to reach its destination. Preaching that is personal and challenging and not vague and abstract will be received. As the early Christian witnesses preached the Good News, their announcement of the presence of the Holy Spirit empowered the embryonic fellowship; a new reincarnation changed them into dynamic centers of personality; the Word became flesh anew. Professor Carl Michalson said, "Preaching recreates the resurrection in the sense that it is always evoking the either/or decision between life and death which is precipitated in the living Lordship of the resurrected one."[9] For some two thousand years, Christians have lectured, preached, and taught about the resurrection of Jesus Christ. Claude Thompson said:

> The temptation is ever with us to adopt the Risen Lord in all sorts of ways. In my college days He was hailed almost in the image of the successful business executive. Later, some people saw Him as a sentimental dreamer. Others wanted to romanticize Him. Educators conspired to instructionalize Him, and now the current fashion of the learned world is to de-mythologize and existentialize Him. We are willing to do almost anything except to worship Him and say: "My Lord and My God!"[10]

It is in the context of Christian worship, and certainly during the preaching time, that the challenge must go out clearly of the necessity for all hearers to affirm the Christ. John Huxtable said, "Christian worship is a dialogue between God and His people, a family conversation in which God discloses himself through the reading of Scriptures and the preaching of the Word, in which the Spirit makes God's activity in an ancient day contemporary with his people in every generation."[11] Rudolph Bultmann places extreme emphasis on preaching when he says, "Christ meets us in the preaching as one crucified and risen. He meets us in the Word of preaching and nowhere else. The faith of Easter is just this—faith in the Word of preaching."[12] The Word of preaching confronts us as the Word of God. This Word questions our accessibility and receptivity, and challenges us to say either "I know not, neither understand I what thou sayest" or "My Lord and My God!" We are asked whether we believe or reject the Word. Bultmann says, "In answering this question, in accepting the Word of preaching as the Word of God and the death and resurrection of Christ as the eschatological event, we are given an opportunity to understand ourselves."[13] And the lamb of Calvary embellishes the privilege of life with opportunities to enjoy all the rich blessings of the Divine. The divine act at Calvary confirms whose I am as a steward and convicts me to say, "My Lord and My God!" It is at this point that the steward recognizes that the time for accountability and responsibility is *now.* Preaching has a tremendous impact on its hearers in all aspects of life.

Carter G. Woodson shared an anecdote that illustrates the effects of preaching on giving:

Returning from the table where he had placed his offering in a church on Sunday morning not long thereafter, this observer saw another striking example of this failure to hit the mark. He stopped to inquire of his friend, Jim Minor, as to why he had not responded to the appeal for a collection. "What!" said Jim, "I ain't givin' that man nothing. That man ain't fed me this morning and I ain't feeding him."[14]

Woodson concluded that these honest and expectant hearers knew nothing new when the preaching event was finished. As one communicant pointed out, "Their wants had not been supplied, and they wondered where they might go to hear a word which had some bearing upon the life which they had to live."[15] C. H. Dodd says, "The preaching of the church is directed toward reconstituting in the experience of individuals the hour of decision which brought Jesus."[16] Likewise, the *Koran* reads:

The test of charity is: do you give something that you value greatly, something that you love? If you give your life in a cause, that is the greatest gift you can give. If you give yourself, that is, your personal efforts, your talents, your skills, your learning, that comes next in degree. If you give your earnings, your property, your possessions, that is also a great gift; for many people love even more than other things. And there are less tangible things, such as position, reputation, the well-being of those we love, the regard of those who can help us, etc. It is unselfishness that God demands and there is no act of unselfishness, however small or intangible but is well within the knowledge of God.[17]

Regardless of the act of charitable stewardship, the Divine is knowledgeable of the gift as well as the attitude of the steward. Critical in being committed to biblical stewardship is the realization that God knows and the steward is accountable not only after death but also right now. Knowing that current stewardship practices have implication for *now* should enhance stewards to give joyously. Rabbinic tradition elaborates the theology of Genesis 22 so that "the emphasis is not so much on the faith and obedience of Abraham as on the voluntary and even joyous self-sacrifice of Isaac."[18] God responded to Abraham's obedience and Isaac's generosity by remembering Israel *now.* Regardless of the place—whether altar of stone, a simple field, or an immaculate sanctuary—during the experience of worship, God demands our best now. Unfortunately, during worship stewardship is represented symbolically by the tithe and offering. We are exhorted to give as the Lord has prospered us. Wouldn't it seem that for us to give less than we should is to offer a blemished sacrifice, to deny the God of Isaac, to dishonor God and make our offering unacceptable? It is at this very moment that the steward stands alone in judgment. John Wesley's famous sermon, "The Great Assize," declares that:

> The Son of man shall bow the sky,
> All nations in that day shall meet,
> Arraign'd at His tremendous bar
> Behold him on his judgment seat.[19]

This text would lead one to believe that judgment is after death or when Christ shall return, and there is validity to this statement. However, judgment is also now, in this age; we are accountable now, as well as afterward. The cross and Resurrection become present realities through preaching; the "eschatological now" is here. "For he says, 'At the acceptable time I have listened to you, and helped you on the day of salvation.' Behold, now is the acceptable time; behold, now is the day of salvation" (2 Corinthians 6:2). Apostolic preaching brings judgment now: "For we are ... to one a fragrance from death to death, to the other a fragrance from life to life" (2 Corinthians 2:15-16).

Nothing can be more final than to know that I live under the daily scrutiny of the risen Christ. This means that in all life's so-called ordinary duties, I stand at the judgment of Christ. As Theo Preiss has so forcefully stated,

> This moment becomes invested with infinite seriousness not only because the time is short and the Parousia is near but because it is loaded with the infinite weight of the mysterious presence in our neighbor of the Son of man and of God himself ...
>
> Man is confronted by his heavenly judge whenever he sees the need of his neighbor; the judgment and the final destiny of each one is in reality decided at the present moment.[20]

Preiss writes in this manner because in the final analysis the only moment we really have is this final moment, the one in which we live and will die. This amplifies the urgency of the message that "today is the acceptable day of the Lord Jesus Christ." Today, not tomorrow or next year, is the day to become a steward of integrity of all resources that the Divine has entrusted for management. Today is the day—now. Claude Thompson said, "It is the meaning of the mission of Jesus, when announcing the approach of the kingdom of God, to make this future at the same time already now a present reality.... Life in the kingdom of God is a present reality."[21] C. H. Dodd used the phrase the "isness of the was" to express the significance of the Christ event and the utter impossibility to confine this act to the first part of the first century. Dodd also used the phrase "realized eschatology" to express the idea of the present reality of the kingdom whereby God acted to establish the kingdom through the advent of Christ.[22]

Stewards are incorporated into the kingdom only in a faith response to a divine action that occurred some two thousand years ago. This divine deed—the Christ Event—to which the *kerygma*—the act of preaching—bears witness, is foundational as it relates to Christendom and to this work, *From Proclamation to Practice*. Preaching is to be a witness of the Christ Event, a divine act actualized and realized in history. Consequently, biblical stewardship preaching is more than "Promotional Sunday" or "Prove-the-Tithe Sunday" or a "Widow's Mite Offering." It is a clarion call for a human response to a divine act. The efficaciousness of this divine act demands a response from the recipients of the kingdom's fruits. Stewards are accountable now, and after death for sure.

Embracing the Word as faithful stewards elevates us from the fear of judgment. As God rewarded Israel because of the obedience of Isaac and faith of Abraham, this "now God" will bless us now and affirm us in the final hour. This phenomenon of "blessing now" is inherent in Bultmann's understanding of "mythology":

> By "mythology" we mean the expression of unobservable realities in terms of observable phenomenon. It is the mode of representation in which the unworldly, the Divine, appears as worldly human, and the other-worldly as this worldly.[23]

Grandmother used to say it like this: "The Lord is blessing me right now, right now. He woke me up this morning and started me on my way. The Lord is blessing me right now." The promise is sure. Reciprocity is divine response to faithful biblical stewards. Speak to us, Brother Malachi:

> Bring the full tithes into the storehouse, that there may be food in my house; and thereby put me to the test, says the Lord of hosts, if I will not open the windows of heaven for you and pour down for you an overflowing blessing (Malachi 3:10).

To receive blessings through the otherworldly Divine via unobservable phenomena necessitates giving to God through the tithe. It is within the context of the *kergyma*, the preaching event, that the otherworldly is humanized and unobservable phenomena become observable reality. How does the Divine pour out blessings? What structures are utilized in pouring out blessings from opened windows in heaven to reach specific destinations? Unobservable phenomena, yet observable reality. Where are the windows of heaven? Otherworldly for sure, yet this-worldly because "he keeps on blessing me." When you say "right now," what determines theorematic truth in monitoring qualitative divine efficacy? Who is qualified to determine the margin of error that negates quantitative blessings? Unobservable phenomena, for sure. However, I know that from somewhere, showers of blessings keep coming my way; the meal barrel still has some meal; the cruet—I checked and it still has oil. Grandmother was right, "The Lord is blessing me right now." All this and more is communicated through the divine-human event of preaching the Word. Again and again, the Word becomes flesh and fortifies faith, blesses blessings, reveals a glimpse of glory, makes assurance blessed, grace amazing, joy unspeakable, and heaven home. It is a genuine challenge to preach the Word through the power of the Holy Spirit knowing of its ability to enhance the quality of life for all of God's children.

Preaching the Word is also a frustrating experience, however, given what we know about the human personality, its fixedness toward permanence and its tenacious cleaving to the familiar. The longer an individual persists in a certain mode, the less likely is radical change. Paul Tillich shares a helpful insight here as he speaks of the need for new life:

> The New Being is not something that simply takes the place of the Old Being. But it is a renewal of the Old which has been corrupted, distorted, split and almost destroyed. But not wholly destroyed. Salvation does not destroy Creation, but it transforms the Old Creation into a New One. Therefore we can speak of the New in terms of re-newal: The threefold "RE," namely, *re*conciliation, *re*union, *re*surrection.[24]

The circus was in town, and grandfather decided he'd take Loston to see the animals, the clowns, enjoy some of the rides and eateries. Loston decided that he wanted to ride on the merry-go-round—and he did, for one solid hour. Grandfather patiently waited and waved. As Loston got off the merry-go-round, he said, "That was fun going round and around." Grandfather, looking into those excited eyes and holding that tender, sticky hand, said, "My boy, you've been gone an hour and spent a whole dollar, but you ain't been nowhere!"

Such innocent joy and tragedy it is, hearing over and over about divine intervention at Calvary for our sins! Calvary, where there was a triune relationship between the Father, the Son, and the Holy Spirit. Calvary, where sin, death, hell, and the grave were conquered. Calvary, where prepentecostalism was conceived. Don't you see how he died at Calvary! Now we enjoy all the fringe benefits of the death, burial, and resurrection of our Lord Jesus Christ, yet we content ourselves to ride on the ecclesiastical merry-go-round for a solid hour, pay our dollar, and say, "That was fun to go round and around; let's do it again next Sunday." Serving the Lord is more than happy rides for a dollar. How can anyone respond to Calvary with any less than offering themselves, their possessions, talents, and resources as committed stewards in the kingdom of God?

All Scripture quotations in this sermon are from the Revised Standard Version of the Bible unless otherwise noted.

The Faithful Steward

W. D. Woods

Let a man so account of us, as of the ministers of Christ, and stewards of the mysteries of God. Moreover it is required in stewards, that a man be found faithful. (1 Corinthians 4:1-2)

The words of our text were written by the apostle Paul to set forth our duty to and respect for ministers of Christ and stewards of the mysteries of God. The apostle calls for the respect due to him and the other apostles, on account of the character and responsibility of their office, which the Corinthians had failed to give.

The precious gifts and authority to preach were from Christ, and not human beings; and they were responsible to him alone for their use and improvement; and by virtue of their high office, they were entitled to the respect and confidence of the people. They shared in the dignity and honor of their Master. Therefore, Paul says, "Let a man so account of us as of the ministers of Christ, and stewards of the mysteries of God."

Though they were but stewards, yet they were not stewards over the common things of this world but of the divine mysteries of God. Their office was above that of a world politician, and the minister that stoops so low as to malign the character of a fellow minister brings a disgrace upon the profession and is not worthy of the respect and confidence of the people—and certainly does not represent Christ, the embodiment of parity.

Ministers have a great trust and for that reason have been appointed masters. Yet they are also servants of the highest rank; they have the care of God's

W. D. Woods was pastor of the Washington Street Baptist Church in Bedford City, Virginia, from 1898 to 1902. This sermon, "The Faithful Steward," was given during a meeting of the Valley Baptist Association around the turn of the century.

household, the responsibility of providing food for the flock. Our Lord's solemn charge to Peter was, "Feed my sheep" (John 21:16-17). In this charge, we see our plain duty, and when we depart from this we cease to do the will of the Master.

Though the writer of these words was not of the original band of apostles, he was divinely appointed to this high office and came to the household of faith as one "born out of due time" (1 Corinthians 15:8). His claim to a place among them was unquestioned. He was divinely ordained and appointed to bring the Gentiles to Christ, hence he gloried in saying, "Unto me, who am less than the least of all saints, is this grace given, that I should preach among the Gentiles the unsearchable riches of Christ; and to make all see what is the fellowship of the mystery, which from the beginning of the world hath been hid in God, who created all things by Jesus Christ: to the intent that now unto the principalities and powers in heavenly places might be known by the church the manifold wisdom of God" (Ephesians 3:8-10).

Under the inspiration of the Holy Spirit, he wrote the words of our text, magnifying the office of a minister of Christ and declaring his independence of all merely worldly considerations and claims. He demands the proper appreciation due the gospel minister and urges faithfulness on the part of those entrusted with the great mission of leading souls to Christ.

Dear fellow ministers, we have in our text a most helpful lesson. If we follow and practice it, we shall meet with greater success in our work for the Master. We have been called and appointed by the Lord Jesus Christ to fill a most important office, to perform a most delicate and onerous piece of work, that is, to stand between heaven and hell and call people to repent of their sins and return to God with faith in Christ and be saved from the destruction of their own vices and sins.

"Moreover, it is required in stewards, that a man be found faithful."

1. Faithful to Christ. Christ gave the apostles their commission; he entrusted them with those most excellent graces and gifts, with which they were to win the world, and said to them, "Occupy until I come."

The minister derives his authority to preach from Christ. His credentials to preach the mysteries of God were given by the great head of the church. Scripture says, "For no man taketh this honor unto himself" (Hebrews 5:4). Christ alone has the authority to cancel this commission.

The message the minister has to deliver is the message of the history of Christ's own life and sacrifice on the cross. Success will attend the efforts only of those who follow his directions and prove faithful to their Master. He plainly says, "Without me you can do nothing" (John 15:5). In his prayer to the Father which he uttered just before his crucifixion, he said, "I have given unto them the words which thou gavest me; and they have received them, and have known surely that I came out from thee, and they have believed that thou didst send me" (John 17:8).

When he sent them out to proclaim the gospel to a lost world, he promised them his perpetual presence. "Go and lo, I am with you ... alway, even unto the end of the world" (Matthew 28:19-20). Through his intercession with the Father, the Holy Spirit was given to them as a completion of their preparation for the great work of saving a lost world.

It is required of stewards to be found faithful—faithful to him who made the appointment and who has power to cancel it at any time; and to him who created the office, for the office is not greater than its creator, nor is the one who fills the position greater than the one who gave the commission.

Stewards of Christ's house are subject to his directions and are morally bound to obey his authority. Christ says, "Ye have not chosen me, but I have chosen you, and ordained you, that ye should go and bring forth fruit, and that your fruit should remain" (John 15:16).

We need his abiding presence to lighten the burden of our crosses, to sweeten the bitter waters of difficulties, to give power and influence to our lives, success to our efforts; for without him we can accomplish nothing.

The great lights that transform our large cities from darkness into day receive their power of illumination from the power house that generates the light. The moment the wire that transmits the electricity is severed, the lights are extinguished and everything is dark and gloomy. So it is with the minister of Christ, who receives power to electrify the human soul from the great power house of God's love. When the cord is cut that connects our lives with that great power house and God's grace, we lose all of our power and the world goes on unheeding our appeals. Our lives become dark and hideous; the human soul indulges in sin without being aroused by our appeals. May God help us to keep in constant communication with heaven, that we may never lose our connection with the Holy Spirit.

Stewards who are faithful to Christ have no time to propagate their own interest or to follow their own fancies. They have not been commissioned to establish their own honor but to foster the kingdom of their Redeemer. They must not require anything without the Master's consent; their work is to spread the eternal truth of salvation. They must appoint what Christ has appointed. They must preach the eternal rules of God's Word and rely solely on God's grace for success, leaving the results with the Lord. Paul says, "By the grace of God I am what I am" (1 Corinthians 15:10). We are witnesses for Christ, to all truth at all times and under all circumstances. Our responsibility is equal to our authority and demands our immediate and careful attention.

How faithful we ought to be to him, who purchased at such a dear cost the right and freedom of a disciple, especially so when the cruel and recreant hirelings are lying around untrue to God and humanity, seeking to gratify their own covetous desires at the expense of our Lord's cause. It is by the almighty grace of Jesus Christ that we make our calling and election sure. We cannot shoulder such grave responsibilities and carry them to a successful termination without the help of an omnipotent God and the directions of the Holy Spirit, especially when iniquities come upon us like a flood and when Satan's devices are so cunning and deceptive.

We must accept our call to this most sacred work with willing hearts and perform most cheerfully the solemn duties attending our mission. By the grace of God we must continue to work faithfully and remain true to our trust until Christ, who appointed us to this high office, shall give us our discharge.

2. Faithful to Proclaim the Mysteries of God. Faithful stewards must teach what Christ has commanded and not the doctrines and comments of human beings. They must not feed the sheep on the chaff of their own petty inventions instead of the pure Word of God. Wholesome Christian doctrine will fatten and stimulate the flock. We must be true to the Lord's flock and feed them on such food that will nourish them up to full stature in Christ Jesus.

We understand by "the mysteries of God" that the infinite personality of God became a revealed presence in Jesus Christ, whose advent into the world was heralded by the angelic host on the plains of Bethlehem. Emerging from the glory he had with the Father before the foundation of the world, the mystery of God appeared and was manifested in the flesh. Human beings beheld the incarnate God as he walked about the plains of Palestine, healing the sick, curing the lepers, giving sight to the blind. Human beings today are looking for the same God because they are afflicted with the same diseases, only more deadly in nature.

The idols of Greece and Rome tottered and fell when the mysteries of God were fully revealed; people renounced the idols they had worshiped and proclaimed their fidelity to God, finding a greater liberty in the truth of God's Son. War's flaming sword hung suspended on the uplifted arm as shepherds listened with joy at the song of the angels, which predicted peace on earth and good will toward all. The star of Bethlehem guided the wise men from the East to the place where the young child lay, that they might behold the revealed mystery of God. By this revelation of divine truth, people have been freed from the fetters of superstition and have thrown aside their idolatrous customs and received greater satisfaction in their sacred devotions to God.

Dear ministers, God has given us the mysteries of his Word to reveal to a lost world lying in wickedness, trespasses, and sin. These mysteries include the entire message of divine truth now revealed in Jesus Christ, embracing all that is truly new to the world in the doctrines of divine revelation, in this age of Christ. They were given to the apostles and their successors to be published to all humanity. "Go ye into all the world, and preach the gospel to every creature" is the Lord's solemn charge (Mark 16:15). We must know the truth and publish it to the world.

The gospel is God's gracious method of recovering the human race from sin and sorrow to holiness and happiness. It is intended to awaken human beings from a slumber of sinful negligence and hold out to them the sceptre of salvation. Therefore it requires that we hold out to them the whole truth under all circumstances.

Abstract meditations and learned research may answer the questions of speculative inquirers and solve intellectual problems, but simpler means are required to save lost souls; immediate access to the world of God must be given to those under the conviction of sin. Science may penetrate the mysteries of nature, sink its shaft deep into the earth and exhume earth's rich treasures; survey the most distant planets, foretell the coming of a comet and going of an eclipse; harness electricity, and make it our servant in a thousand different ways. Science may with its powerful penetrating force look far into the heavens, but it is not able, neither will it ever be able, to satisfy the cravings of the human soul or answer the all-important question: "What must I do to be saved?"

Philosophy has taught us many important truths and maxims, but it has never taught us how to die. Medicine has offered many wonderful cures for the human system but has never prescribed the remedy to cure the sick soul. "Believe on the Lord Jesus Christ" and "By grace ye are saved" are the only prescriptions that have cured every penitent soul.

These are the remedies we must as faithful stewards prescribe for our patients. By faithful exposition of the truth, we shall arrest the attention of the careless and indifferent ones, interest those inclined to hear, and impress the soul with the importance of salvation. Human sluggishness demands a stimulus, and human infirmity a help; this necessity of human weakness is met in the wise economy of God's plan of salvation.

God has ordained and appointed us from the foundation of the world to the high office of stewards and commanded us to be faithful in discharging our duties, that all may hear the joyful news of salvation and accept God's gracious offer.

The doctrines of divine revelation are unfathomable mysteries; no plumb line of human reason has ever sounded their depths. They are like the great ocean—we may walk along its shores or plunge into its transcendent depths or gaze upon its clear waters that mirror every star, or sail across its vast expanse, only to realize what profound depths have we left unsounded or undiscovered, what mountains and valleys have we left unexplored. It is even so with the mysteries of God's Word.

We may behold the prophecies of the Old Testament, or follow the lowly Nazarene as he walked under the bending palms of Palestine. We may look with horror upon the rugged brow of Calvary, and accompany the women to the sepulchre and behold the empty tomb; or mount the alpine peaks of the revelations and imagine we have learned or fathomed the mysteries of God's holy Word. Yet how many broad fields of God's truths are left unexplored, how many mysteries unsolved! But if we have been faithful and followed the directions of the Holy Spirit, we can say as Job did in the days of old, "But the thunder of his power who can understand?" (Job 26:14). And some imprisoned soul will find its way into the glorious liberty of Jesus Christ by the little we have revealed.

Oh, fellow ministers, let us as faithful stewards stand on the walls of Zion and declare the whole counsel of God until the world shall be reclaimed for our Redeemer.

He who rules over the destiny of us all, to whom all power in heaven and earth is given, himself became the end of the law for righteousness to everyone who believes.

3. Faithful to the Charge over Which God Has Called Us. Our Lord entrusted the flock to Peter, to feed and nourish them on the Word of God. So precious were their souls that Jesus would not leave the care of the sheep to Peter until he had put him through a most rigid examination and extorted three solemn declarations to prove his fidelity.

Jesus has such tender regard for the sheep that he could not leave them to unfaithful hands, and especially to those who do not love him—because those who do not love the Master will never love and care for the flock. Nothing but constraining love will make us brave the difficulties that confront Christian ministers today.

Christ has committed the saving of the world to his disciples and has taken his departure to heaven to wait the results of our labors, keeping a constant watch over those he has left behind, helping us to gather in lost and wandering ones. The apostle Paul outlines our work when taking his final departure for Jerusalem: "Take heed therefore unto yourselves, and to all the flock, over the which the Holy Ghost hath make you overseers, to feed the church of God, which he hath purchased with his own blood" (Acts 20:28).

The faithful minister, like the Master, must keep a constant watch over the sheep and have a tender regard for the weak and feeble ones, especially those who are under his or her immediate charge. Take care of all the flock, that none wander from the fold and be devoured by some ravenous beast.

It is the duty of the shepherd to feed all the sheep and lead them into the green pastures of God's Word. It is our duty to lay meat before them, that the weak may become strong, and to do what we can to heal the distempered ones. We must feed them on wholesome Christian doctrine and correct them with a tender evangelical discipline and see that nothing is wanting to nourish them up to eternal life.

We are not only to feed those within, but to bring to those without. The faithful steward must ever consider the interest of the Master; from him we received the trust, and to him we must render an account of stewardship. The church is his by right of purchase. He bought it with a great price, even his own blood; therefore it is dear to him and should demand our most faithful care and attention.

This a glorious work; it is an honorable work. It is one in which angels have been denied the honor of engaging, a work in which the good of each has been engaged. It is so glorious and important that heaven rejoices more over one sinner that repents than over ninety-nine joyous persons who need no repentance. It is a work which God the Father takes a deep interest in, which was manifested in the gift of his Son to the world to suffer an ignominious death on the rugged cross.

It is right that we should take delight in a work which the immaculate Lamb spent a life of toil and persecution and suffered a shameful death at the hands of murderers. The Holy Spirit accompanies those who are ministering to the saints and impresses the gospel upon their hearts. Surely if there is anything on earth that should solicit our earnest attention, our greatest effort, and our deepest interest, it should be the work of ministering to the flock of God.

Medical practitioners spend year after year studying their profession in order to become acquainted with the human system, with the various ills that assail the human body, and with the remedies best calculated to remove these ills. That they may amass a fortune, excel in their profession, and bless the human race, they burn the midnight oil and become conversant with the greatest minds.

Why should not we, the messengers of Christ, seeking lost souls and with eternal things in our charge, be equally—nay, more—earnest in turning sinners from eternal damnation to the celestial city, whose gates stand ajar to bid them welcome. We should magnify our office, discharge faithfulness to every duty. "Moreover it is required in stewards, that a man be found faithful."

Our calling transcends all others, as the soul does that of the body; and the things of eternity, as those of time. Not even the queen on her gorgeous throne, nor the president in the executive mansion, has the honor of occupying a position equal to that of a minister of the gospel. Let every duty sink into the shade by the side of our work for God and humanity.

The great apostle to the Gentiles says, "I count all things but loss for the excellency of the knowledge of Christ Jesus my Lord: for whom I have suffered the loss of all things, and do count them but dung, that I may win Christ" (Philippians 3:8). The work Christ has assigned him was uppermost in his soul, and his chief ambition was to finish the work of his ministry, that he might receive the crown of life.

This should be the chief desire of every faithful servant: to bring others to Christ. Human beings are without God and going away from God, and hence must be turned to God with all of their heart, that they may seek him while he may be found, and call upon him while he is near.

I need not point you to heathen lands, where millions worship at heathen shrines; but let me tell you that thousands in our own immediate communities are living in unrighteousness, and vast multitudes are buried in sin and trespasses and must be awakened from a sinful stupor and brought to Christ. Their misery is so great that they call for the loudest sympathy.

Brothers and sisters, it is an awful thing to let others die in a state of damnation. We must hasten to gather them into the "Gospel Ark" or they will be lost forever; whatever we neglect, it should not be those under the curse of the Law.

We must run as Aaron did with the censer and stand between the living and the dead, that this death plague of damnation may be stayed until we can gather the lost and wandering into the fold. May God help us to summon all of our energies in the Master's cause and start out in this noble work of rescuing the perishing and care for the dying.

There is work enough to employ all of our talents and time. It is surprising how some in the ministry have time to devote to other callings and professions, while all who are truly interested in the work of saving souls feel that if they could have a hundred days for one, a hundred talents for one, they could employ all in the work of ministry and then leave as much undone! Have you any spare time, or talents unemployed? The wide world is before you in which to employ them. If you cannot climb the rugged mountains, you can stand in the valley and by word or song cheer the struggling multitudes as they ascend the lofty peaks. If you cannot sail the boisterous ocean among the swiftest of the fleet, you can help to launch the vessel that will save a drowning one. If you cannot fight in the thick of the battle, you can go when the war is over and care for the dying or cover the dead. Do not stand idly by, stewards of the living God, and see your brothers and sisters perish beneath the tempestuous waves of eternal ruin.

4. The Reward of the Faithful. Our Lord offered a never-fading crown to those who remain faithful to the end. "Be faithful until death, and I will give you the crown of life," says Christ (Revelation 2:10, RSV).

This life of toil and warfare shall end shortly in eternal joy and rest for the soul. The ransomed of the Lord shall return and come to Zion to serve and worship God in the church triumphant. They shall come with song and praise in their mouths; sorrow and sighs shall be made to flee away by the divine consolations.

They that have mourned in carrying out our Lord's blessed commands are blessed, for they shall be comforted. They that have been faithful over a few things shall be rulers over many; they shall come to heaven singing the song that no one can learn but the redeemed of the Lord. When they shall enter into the joy of their Lord, it shall be everlasting joy, without any mixture of sorrow.

It shall not only fill our hearts to their perpetual satisfaction, but it shall be upon our heads as an ornament of grace and a crown of glory, and as a garland worn in token of our victory over the great enemy of our souls. "There we shall obtain joy and gladness, which we could never expect to obtain this side of heaven, and we shall cease from troubling, and the weary are at rest." Amen.

All Scripture quotations in this sermon are from the King James Version of the Bible unless otherwise noted.

Where Your Treasure Is

Ella Pearson Mitchell

"For where your treasure is, there will your heart be also." (Matthew 6:21)

Here we are at the close of our annual stewardship effort, and since it is also near the close of the year, this *could* be the very climax of our spiritual calendar. But I just read somebody's mind. It was saying, "Pleas and pledges aren't hardly shouting material. How on earth does this get to be the peak of our spiritual year?" Well, I leave it to Jesus to answer that one: "Where your treasure is, there will your heart be also." In the words of our streets, "Put your money where your mouth is, and that will tell us if your heart matches your mouth." If Jesus is "Lord of my life," as we so glibly say, could this be the time we've anxiously awaited so we could supremely demonstrate our love for God?

Maybe we'd better look in greater depth at Jesus' striking statement. It comes from his Sermon on the Mount. This sixth chapter of Matthew flows smoothly from prayer and fasting, to piety, to possessions.

The first thing we see on possessions is that this earth is not a safe place to keep the main ones. When Jesus talks of moths eating up cloth, I think he's referring to more than clothing. I think they hoarded yard goods like my African friends and I do. And he is saying that this is a poor savings strategy. One moth hole in the wrong place, and the whole bolt may be destroyed.

Again, steel may seem eternal, but rust gets to it. When we lived in Richmond, a bridge a few feet from our home had to be entirely rebuilt. It *looked*

Ella Pearson Mitchell is visiting professor of homiletics at the Interdenominational Theological Center in Atlanta and leads workshops and seminars with her husband, Henry. She has served as director of continuing education at the Virginia Union School of Theology and dean of chapel at Spelman College.

strong, but it was shockingly rotted out by rust. America could stop the recession tomorrow if we could find the funds to pay for repairing all our rusted bridges. Rust and termites and hurricanes are all hard on structures. It does not appear that these are the best investment either.

Then Jesus warned about thieves breaking through and stealing. Houses in his day were easy to break and enter. We have better security now—brick walls and iron window grates. But today's thieves do not break houses, they break laws; and what they steal may or may not be replaced by the government. With interest at the bottom and bank laws like they are, even cash money presents problems as a way to get secure.

Money isn't safe in our own hands; we will always have to put it somewhere. A couple dear to me put theirs in some real estate which just boomed and flourished for years. So they rolled it over into more real estate. But suddenly the need for their apartments disappeared. The people moved away, and all of their equity in hundreds of units evaporated overnight. They lost it all.

Now, of course, I'm not saying that all investments are unsafe. What Jesus is saying is simply that human hearts and souls dare not be attached too closely to material things of *any* kind. Jesus is advising us not to invest in or identify our most important treasures with what can be handled and counted here on this planet. Rather, he advises storing things in heaven, where they will be safe. But, of course, you are wondering just where the teller is for these deposits. And I owe it to you to reveal that the treasures are invested here, in the work of the kingdom here, but the records of the deposits are kept in heaven.

When I recall my dear friends who lost it all, this statement may make more sense. You see, I don't think they gave away very much when they were rolling their gains over and reinvesting their profits. And yet, if they had helped some of the causes they ignored, at least that much would now still be to their credit. At least that much would still provide lasting satisfaction. And if somebody had to help them, they could at least think of it as bread cast upon the water. The records are in heaven, but any benefits needed are safely waiting to be passed out down here.

This may be a brand new insight to us ordinary, wage-earning Christians, but it is well-respected, hard data among those who are both wealthy and Christian. They hire people to tell them how best to give for tax purposes, all the while knowing that they are also laying up some treasure in heaven. For them, there is no question that these are their best investments.

I will always remember the plaque I used to read in the entrance to the chapel at Colgate Rochester Divinity School. The donor was a former candle-maker named Sam Colgate. He kept adding to his contributions in multiples of the tithe. God blessed him greatly, but of all that he received, only the things he gave away remain to this day.

Whether investment is safe or not, however, is not the main issue. All of this has undertones of self-interest. The real issue raised by our text is, Where is your heart? What does your soul crave most? *That* is your most valued possession or your most important goal. Jesus says in the text that wherever our most valued possessions are, that is where our hearts are. Or we can turn it around and say that where our hearts are will be revealed by what we value most. It seems a truism, a fact so obvious as not to matter. But when suddenly we apply it to material things, it stings. It says that money (or property) and love (or faith) are inescapably bound together.

When I was a girl, during the Great Depression, there was a popular song which alleged, "I can't give you anything but love, baby." Times were tough, and it seemed plausible enough on the surface—that is, until you watched a person who really loved. You see, if that person had *anything* of this world's goods with which to survive, real love would have insisted on sharing *something*. Real love is like that.

A diary may describe love in poetic terms to stir the heart, but the most accurate index of true love is the personal checkbook. It says in incontrovertible terms where the writer's heart is. Sure, you have rent and utilities and health insurance. And of course you have car payments and clothing and food to care for. But love, as we say, will find a way.

Lovers of God and God's kingdom will look at disposable income and find a way. They will insist on a gift to God that is worthy of the love they bear. If there is not enough disposable, after necessities, they will look at the so-called necessities. They will look at the size of cars and houses, the wardrobe and the freezer, and ask, "Have I lived too high on the hog and squeezed God out?" When you understand this, you will understand how it is that seniors with fixed low incomes often give the most.

Back in 1954 my husband and I bought a long-desired station wagon. It was just wonderful, but after four months we realized that those $156 monthly payments were more than we could bear. We decided to unload it, but a loved one objected. She said it would make people think we were in trouble financially. So what? The truth was that we were! She didn't come right out and say it, but it was obvious that one way to keep the car would have been to apply our tithe to our car payments instead. We respectfully declined the advice and traded the car for a dependable junker. I shall never forget the relief, and neither of us ever regretted it. That unloading was one of the greatest spiritual blessings of our lives. In time, our finances changed for the better, but our love for the things of God never changed. Love is like that.

This is not at all unusual. All the people I know who really love the Lord and systematically tithe are actually happy that they follow this order of priorities. I have yet to find an ex-tither; if they give to God's work out of love and faith, they never tire of giving and serving. They only wish they had more to give.

In the late forties we lived up the hill from a new race track built on the mud flats of San Francisco Bay, beside the city of Berkeley. The bus stop nearest to the track was a block from our housing-project apartment. It was common to see people begging for a dime for bus fare home. They had spent all they had on bets on the horses, but none ever seemed to complain; they only wished they had had more to "give" at the track.

My husband preached about this one Sunday, but we forgot about it after that. Twenty years later, after a funeral in East Oakland, we were stopped at the door. We were in a hurry to get to the airport, but this couple seemed so anxious to talk that we yielded and listened. They recalled my husband's sermon about the gamblers who only regretted that they didn't have more to bet. They reported that they had decided not to be outdone by gamblers, and they rejoiced that they had been tithers ever since that day over twenty years before. Their heart was clearly in it, and their gifts were a joy indeed.

Let me share about one other person who didn't regret systematic stewardship. Our church had abolished all tickets and "drives" and adopted the every-member canvass. Some sisters were very unhappy about no tickets and cooking; we had taken away their most treasured way of "serving the Lord." A year later they organized a move to go back to the old way. In the discussion, one of the deacons arose and testified: "I have been a Christian for fifty years, and I have always served the Lord with joy. But I have never, ever, given so much as I now give, and I have never enjoyed it more. I am delighted not to have to deal with ticket sellers every Sunday, and I can't tell you how happy I am to direct a Sunday school whose every need is already in a fully funded budget. I refuse to go back to Egypt!" As he sat down, the church applauded. As a result, the sisters cooked *free* dinners, gladly funded by a church with love for God and for fellowshiping with each other. Their hearts were in a good place, and it showed.

A friend of ours named Raymond Rasberry has summed up our lesson in a beautiful song. It affirms the lasting quality of our loving offerings to the Lord:

> You may build great cathedrals large or small,
> You can build skyscrapers grand and tall,
> You may conquer all the failures of the past,
> But only what you do for Christ will last.
>
> Remember only what you do for Christ will last;
> Remember only what you do for Christ will last;
> Only what you do for Him will be counted at the end,
> Only what you do for Christ will last![1]

All Scripture quotations in this sermon are from the King James Version of the Bible unless otherwise noted.

What Is This I Hear?

William J. Shaw

And he said also unto his disciples, There was a certain rich man, which had a steward; and the same was accused unto him that he had wasted his goods. And he called him, and said unto him, How is it that I hear this of thee? give an account of thy stewardship; for thou mayest be no longer steward. (Luke 16:1-2)

The issue of stewardship within or without the Christian faith will forever be a muddled matter so long as it is a subject for human reason's resolution rather than an expression of the divine-human relationship. We would do well to hear the unqualified voice of authority in this area. If we are authentic followers of Jesus, how can we do anything else? Luke states that he spoke to "his disciples." Listen to the Master: "There was a certain rich man, which had a steward . . ."

Whenever God is imaged, we always behold One who is rich. He is the God of *excessively more than "enough."* There is no lack in God. With God there is always sufficiency—*and more.* Indeed, the God of Bible revelation is not just the God of sufficiency and more but the God of all things and everything.

The riches of God are not to be measured merely by their all-inclusive quantity, but ought to be conceived of by and for their incomparable quality. In fact, the quality of everything is enhanced simply because all that is belongs to the One who is infinitely rich. How the human ego rejoices with pride to say

William J. Shaw is pastor of the White Rock Baptist Church, Philadelphia, Pennsylvania. He serves as president of the Metropolitan Christian Council of Philadelphia and director of the Ministers' Division of the National Congress of Christian Education. He serves on several civic and religious boards in the Philadelphia area.

that a certain rich man owns or uses "this thing" or "that thing." God spoke to Peter to correct him and to inform all others who hear or read that nothing that he has touched should be considered common (of no value) or unclean (corrupting in itself). Because everything has value, it would follow that everything should be handled with care.

For the common person, those who are rich are usually remote and inaccessible. Not so, however, with God. Whenever and wherever the God of Scripture is imaged, God is in relationship. Our God is never a God in isolation, a God in solitary existence. God is not known through abstract contemplation, though God does challenge the mind and nourish the spirit. Rather is the God of our faith known as a God in relationship: "There was a certain rich man, which had a steward."

Note that this relationship is depicted as a relationship of God to and with a person—he had a steward. The wonder of this person-to-person relationship can't be fully appreciated when it is given single depiction. The Bible casts the relationship in more than one modality. Our very being as persons is derived from God. The "Book of Beginnings" says that God created us in his own image, male and female he created us (Genesis 1:27). Our personhood is his creation. Elsewhere our personhood is related to the Divine as a child to the Father: "A certain man had two sons" (Luke 15:11). Here in our text the relationship is that of the Divine to a person who has access to the Divine's possessions—a steward. In fact, this person has more than mere access to—he also has a delegated control of and authority over—the possessions of the Divine. He has the responsibility of using those possessions not merely to preserve what is but to secure gain for the Divine.

What a staggering thought! God trusts the steward with the management of his resources! Who is this steward? In the context of the creation story, each one of us is to see ourself as the individual of entrustment: Adam is you. The Lukan text singularizes the person of the text, but not to point out one or even some and then to excuse all the rest. The identity of the steward is singularized so that there would be purposeful narrowing of focus. The individual is the steward. The believer is the bailiff. In the context of resurrection reality, the steward of holy trust is the church, of which the believer is a member.

What are the Master's goods which we have in trust? What have we received from the Lord that we are to use for his glory and according to his interest? 'Tis clear, according to the Scripture, that we have received our being "in his image" as a trust: life itself. The very character of our being—"male and female created he them"—affirms our sexuality; it is the work of God, not a deed of the devil. It is a work setting forth the necessity of our life in relationship to others—male and female—as a relationship designed for the completion and fulfillment of individual selves. It is not good for the self to be alone. We have received in trust life in community.

What are the Master's goods that we have in trust? They are the whole of God's creation, the things God has made: the earth, fields and streams, the harvest of soil and sea, the beauty of sky and atmosphere. They are the skills of science and the abilities to develop economic and financial structures and resources. They are the riches of the created kingdom, the world.

What are the Master's goods that we have in trust? They are the vision and Good News of the glorious gospel of Jesus Christ given to the church to proclaim and, by the Holy Spirit, to manifest throughout the world—with no area exempt. The Master's "goods" are the ministry of the unsearchable riches of Jesus Christ intended for and accessible to all persons by faith.

What an entrustment! What a disposition of the Divine to place his resources into the hands of his stewards—into your hands, into our hands.

Alas! A voice arrests us. The rich man speaks: "What is this I hear?" The steward stands accused. Who are our accusers, and what is the substance of the accusation? The charge is one of waste, of mismanagement. The accuser is not identified in the text, but the source must be more than that of mere rumor. God is too just to call us to account on the basis of rumor. Nay, 'tis the rumble of the results of our mismanagement that cries out to the Father's ear. 'Tis the tug and tear at the heart of God occasioned by our use of God's resources that causes him to inquire of us. A truth of the divine-human relationship is that the Almighty has made himself vulnerable, liable by our use of that which belongs to him. The image of God among us is an image which, in many ways, the steward shapes. The attitude of others to the Divine is deeply influenced by the steward's doings. The quality of human relationships is impacted greatly by the steward's faithfulness.

"What is this I hear?" Do we detect an echo of hurt in the voice of God: "*How* is it that I hear *this* of *thee?*" *This*—waste! *This*—mismanagement! *This*—nonuse! *This*—misdirected use! *This*—utilization as though it were your own!

"How is it that I hear this of *thee*—you of all people?" You—with whom I have entered into a relationship of trust. You—whom I have placed in a position of prominence and authority, of access and responsibility. What reason have you to do this to me with that which is mine?

Do we detect here also a harbinger of divine wrath over the possible misuse of God's goods? Do we not see even the inevitable reality of judgment? Produce your account, for you may no longer be a steward.

"Give an account of thy stewardship." Ever must we remember that we are accountable, answerable to God. Were our stewardship to be summoned before God for judgment, would the charge of waste be sustained?

What of our being in God's image? Does our life as sexual beings reflect the harmony and wholeness that God designed? Or have we misused it to exploit and deny the personhood of the other? to distort and destroy life in community? to engage in narrowing and negating self-love to the detriment of other-love? Has our life in community been one of justice and caring or of mistreatment and coldness? Has our human sexuality been an instrument of holy creation of life where new life is birthed into a covenant of love and nurturing, of committed pairing and caring as man and woman, husband and wife, father and mother? Or has that sexuality been an instrument of unloved birth, unnurtured and unsupported life settings?

What have we done with our Lord's goods? What is it to waste them? to mismanage them? Is it not to utilize them for ends other than the common good and God's glory? Is it not to pollute the air and the streams? Is it not to destroy the mutually supported relationships of creation's matter? Is it not to build economic and financial structures that oppress people, making them poor, while at the same time accumulating in the coffers of a few mammoth wealth, causing them to think they rival God?

Is it not waste to allow God's resources to remain unused in the face of human need, unused in corporate, governmental, and personal treasuries and bins while countless live in lack? Is it not mismanagement to deny divine ownership of all of earth's resources and to treat them as if they are wholly our own? to separate money from faith, giving from faith's mandate, and guidelines for its use from divine concern? Is it not mismanagement to utilize earth's wealth with no reference to God's will? Is it not gross mismanagement to make goods into our god?

What have we done as a faith community with the gospel of the kingdom of God? Have we not been charged to bear its tidings to the ends of the earth, to all peoples and systems of the earth? Christ has promised that if he were lifted up, he would draw all people unto himself (John 12:32). Is the decline of church membership in some settings a negative reflection on the magnetism of Christ or a declaration that we have wasted this power by placing something or someone else at the center of attention? Does the cry of dereliction and despair heard on our city streets and from our prisons accuse us before the Divine? Where is the presence and possibility of the kingdom of God in evidence if not in the church of our Lord Jesus Christ? Where is the vision of hope believed and the voice of hope heralded?

We have such a world-changing power present to us, ready to dwell within us and to work through us. It is not waste to be open to it, to be submissive before it, indeed, to be joyful in it.

"What is this I hear?" Will the Lord be pleased with what he hears? with what he sees when our stewardship accounts are presented to him?

It is sobering that, at the moment of his summons, there seems to be the realization on the part of the steward that all that he has been managing does indeed belong to the "rich man" and that he does have a just interest in what has been and is being done with his goods. Feeling the inevitability of a negative judgment upon his stewardship, and recognizing that he has in fact no personal, independent base of support and resource, he frantically tries to actualize in fact that which he has attitudinally affirmed and practiced: a separated and sufficient stance from the owner. What folly!

Commended for his belated effort to utilize his Master's goods to the benefit of others, the steward is nonetheless condemned for trying to do the impossible—to live with divided loyalties, to acknowledge God as owner while denying the status of the self as accountable steward.

"What is this I hear?" The noise of a cover-up? the rustle of efforts at evasion? It won't work! The record is too clear. It can't be erased. God can't be deceived.

Far better is it that the Divine should hear the voice of confession—that we should confess to God our unfaithfulness, our waste and mismanagement, our resolve by God's Spirit that we will be wasteful no longer. To waste the Lord's goods is to waste our lives. To fail to manage to his gain and glory is to simultaneously manage to our loss. If we confess our sins, God is ready and willing to forgive us our sins.

It pleased God to relate to us in the holy bonds of entrustment. It is not God's will thereby to deprive us of or deny us any good thing. Faithfulness to and in our trust increases our blessings. Accountability in our stewardship increases the dimensions and opportunities of our stewardship. Faithfulness in our stewardship of the goods of God opens to us by grace the doors through which we can share in the glories of God.

"He that is faithful in that which is least is faithful also in much. . . . If therefore ye have not been faithful in the unrighteous mammon, who will commit to your trust the true riches?" (Luke 16:10-11).

All Scripture quotations in this sermon are from the King James Version of the Bible unless otherwise noted.

An Act of Charity Toward the Rich

James A. Forbes, Jr.

Now the company of those who believed were of one heart and soul, and no one said that any of the things which he possessed was his own, but they had everything in common. And with great power the apostles gave their testimony to the resurrection of the Lord Jesus, and great grace was upon them all. There was not a needy person among them, for as many as were possessors of lands or houses sold them, and brought the proceeds of what was sold and laid it at the apostles' feet; and distribution was made to each as any had need. Thus Joseph who was surnamed by the apostles Barnabas (which means, Son of encouragement), a Levite, a native of Cyprus, sold a field which belonged to him, and brought the money and laid it at the apostles' feet.

But a man named Ananias with his wife Sapphira sold a piece of property, and with his wife's knowledge he kept back some of the proceeds and brought only a part and laid it at the apostles' feet. But Peter said, "Ananias, why has Satan filled your heart to lie to the Holy Spirit and to keep back part of the proceeds of the land? While it remained unsold, did it not remain your own? And after it was sold, was it not at your disposal? How is it that you have contrived this deed in your heart? You have not lied to men but to God." When Ananias heard these words, he fell down and died. And great fear

---

James A. Forbes, Jr., is the fifth senior minister to serve the Riverside Church in New York City. Before assuming this position, he was the Joe R. Engle Professor of Preaching at Union Theological Seminary, New York City, and on the teaching staff at Auburn Theological Seminary. He also has served as director of education at Interfaith Metropolitan Theological Education, Inc., in Washington, D.C. He is well known throughout the United States and Canada as a preacher and conference leader.

---

came upon all who heard of it. The young men rose and wrapped him up and carried him out and buried him.

After an interval of about three hours his wife came in, not knowing what had happened. And Peter said to her, "Tell me whether you sold the land for so much." She said, "Yes, for so much." But Peter said to her, "How is it that you have agreed together to tempt the Spirit of the Lord? Hark, the feet of those that have buried your husband are at the door, and they will carry you out." Immediately she fell down at his feet and died. When the young men came in they found her dead, and they carried her out and buried her beside her husband. And great fear came upon the whole church, and upon all who heard of these things. (Acts 4:32–5:11)

A strange thing happened in the New Testament Christian community one day. In the space of three hours, two of the wealthiest members fell dead at the feet of the apostle Peter and were buried next to each other. They were a husband-and-wife team. This sermon is about how this tragedy took place, but more particularly, about what the events of that day say to Christians in our time.

To get the point it is necessary to read the story as it is recorded in Acts 4:32–5:11 (see above). From this account it seems that the early church was characterized by a spirit of generosity. At least for a brief period the spirit of Jubilee was strong. It seemed the year of release had finally come. The Resurrection, the Ascension, and Pentecost had taken place and a new community was formed, dedicated to living in the Spirit of the Lord.

Apostles who had spent much time with Jesus taught others what they could remember about the "good life" according to Jesus. Members of the fellowship visited from house to house. They broke bread together, received instructions from the apostles, and were nourished in the spirit of prayer.

A most unusual feature of the new community was the way they shared their resources. Their readiness to sacrifice whatever they had led Luke to make the extraordinary claim that those who believed were of one heart and soul, and none of them said that any of the things they possessed were their own, but "they had everything in common." Nobody suffered for lack of basic needs, because property owners were willing to sell houses and land. The proceeds were turned over to the apostles for distribution as needs became known.

What a heart-warming moment it was when Barnabas, a Levite, a native of Cyprus, came forward in the assembly to present the proceeds from the sale of the field that belonged to him. How encouraging! How inspiring! Even the angels in heaven must have been impressed with this spirit of sacrifice. Surely the spirit of the self-giving Christ was alive and well in this band of baptized believers.

A Tragic Fate

But there was a man named Ananias, who, with his wife, Sapphira, sold a piece of property and with her full knowledge withheld some of the proceeds. The text tells us of this couple's tragic fate. And certainly all who witnessed this event were left awestruck.

I have noticed in this text what may have been a flaw in the behavior of this Christian fellowship. It is not the primary concern of the text, but it stands out because it says something about the attitudes of people who are the beneficiaries of the resources of the rich, as well as those of means.

Do we really care for those persons of means who are supportive of us, or is it primarily their largess that concerns us?

Now, don't get me wrong. I have no intention of justifying greed or protecting the rich from any appropriate critique. In fact, this message will challenge Christians, rich and poor—and those in between.

One thing that concerns me about this text is the fact that nobody seemed to care enough to find Sapphira and warn her about the strange and tragic events of that day. There was a three-hour period in which someone might have found a way to inform her of the death of her husband and the circumstances that led to his untimely demise. Don't you agree that someone should have made contact with her? Is that too much to ask? I call it an act of charity toward the rich.

Did they send someone to her house? Maybe they didn't know where she lived. We know that most of them were poor. Did Ananias and Sapphira live in a secluded or exclusive section of town? Even if they couldn't find her, the ushers at the door could have whispered a word of warning. And even if she slipped into the assembly before they could get to her, wouldn't it have been the Christian thing to do to stop her from giving too quick an answer to Peter. Shouldn't someone have shouted to her, "Wait, Sapphira! Think before you speak!"

The reason I'm sensitive about this is because I've noticed how we treat persons of means. Those of us who have development responsibilities look at them with dollar signs in our eyes. We see them primarily as benefactors, failing to raise the question of how the needy can also benefit those who support our institutions. So I thought I ought to call us "money raisers" to cultivate the capacity to engage in acts of charity toward the rich. There is one specific ministry in our text in which we can share. It is at the heart of the faith and serves as a challenge for each and every member of the fellowship of Jesus' followers.

If someone had found Sapphira and told her about the strange happenings that had taken place, she would have been in a state of shock. But later, she probably would have asked, "What does this all mean? What message is the Spirit trying to teach us?" What answer would you give her? What is the theological significance of the fatal occurrence?

I remember one preacher's interpretation of the text with which I take serious exception. An evangelist had come to conduct a revival at a church that I was pastoring in Richmond, Virginia. The preacher had a special gift for discerning character flaws. In the early part of the revival, he announced that someone was guilty of infidelity. A deacon came forward and slumped to the floor. We thought he had died! The evangelist laid hands on him and the deacon was revived. Even I became intimidated for fear that I had forgotten some past impropriety.

As I stood to present him, I said, "I will not give lengthy remarks because I do not want to get in the way of the Spirit ..." The speaker got up immediately and put his hand on my shoulder and said, "But yea, thou art in the way, said the Lord ..." I nearly froze in my tracks as I waited for the revelation of some shameful secret. But he went on to complete his sentence, "... because I have placed you in the way to be a leader to my people." Whee! What a relief from temporary paralysis!

On the final night of the revival, he preached on the story of Ananias and Sapphira. He said that the Lord demands all. Anything less than giving all leads to eventual death. Persons in the church who call themselves Christians, he said, who have never experienced giving all are at the edge of the grave. At the end of the sermon, he asked the ushers to lock the door. "This is the time to act on the gospel you have heard," he exhorted. "Bring forth your billfolds and purses and empty the entire contents on the communion table. Only in this way will you demonstrate radical trust that is demanded of mature Christians. You've got to give all. Don't be like Ananias and Sapphira and hold back part of what you have."

What a heavy moment it was! People were intimidated into giving out of fear of imminent death. People came forward, and many gave all they had. I felt that I was asking for the loss of my life by saving some of my money in case some of them needed money to get home from the service. After the collection of money, the preacher asked if there were persons who had pressing financial needs. He invited several persons (but not very many) to come forward and take what they needed from the common collected treasury.

Now you can see why I consider it a must to get our theology straight before we start interpreting the moral of the story. In the light of this gross misinterpretation I've just described, it becomes your responsibility not to let anyone intimidate you into an understanding that violates your sensitivity. With this word of caution, let me offer another approach to the message of our text.

Persisting Predicament

I think I understand what might have motivated Ananias and Sapphira. Perhaps they felt that with everybody giving so freely, someone should hold on to something for the rainy day. People were caught up in expectation of the early return of the Lord. A kind of interim ethic ensued. What would happen if Jesus delayed his coming? With all the widows and orphans joining the church, someone had better reserve a cushion for the season of dashed hopes.

But there is a larger picture. I think I observe in this passage the projection of an ideal arrangement. If one reads the Bible from Genesis to Revelation, a certain sense of how our resources should be managed begins to emerge. God makes provisions for the needs of all the people. The people, when they act according to God's will, share with each other as one body, heart, and mind.

In our text, Luke captures this ideal. His description of the early church is designed to remind us that when things are as God wills, and when the day of Jubilee has come, when the day of redistribution has come, people will not hoard their resources.

No one will be able to relax and sit on his or her riches until all have had their basic needs adequately met. Does this sound like an accurate description of the ideal arrangement from a biblical perspective? I believe it is the challenge presented to each person of faith. We are encouraged in our lifestyles to live out evidence that God is infinitely trustworthy, can sustain our lives, provide for our security, and even, if we die, can raise us to the full abundance of life of which Jesus spoke.

Our text goes on to paint the picture of a persisting predicament in human communities. There is in all of us—rich and poor—a human longing to be seen in the best light. Don't you strive to project yourself in the best possible light?

So when Barnabas sells his land and brings his money and puts it at the apostles' feet, I do not know what the ritual of renunciation looked like, but I can imagine it was a great moment. They must have sung a hymn of praise, and Peter must have looked very approvingly upon Barnabas as he knelt there. It almost was as if this man responded to an altar call: "All to Jesus I surrender."

Ananias and Sapphira, who are used to being on the top of every consideration, and whose resources allowed them to be the best at whatever they wanted, simply couldn't stand seeing someone else manifest a level of maturity in the faith that exceeded theirs. The applause, the approving eye of Peter and the people, stirred up their longing to appear in the best light.

But another part of this persisting predicament is true for all of us as well. While we have a longing to appear in the best light, we often are unwilling to pay the price for the appearance. In my home state of North Carolina, the motto was *"Esse Quam Vederum"*—to be rather than to seem. Nevertheless we are often quite willing to seem, even if we can't pull off the being part.

There also is a tendency, as Lewis Smedes of Fuller Seminary once said, to sacrifice radical consciousness of truth for the sake of security. That is to say that when your security is at stake, you tend to lose the clear focus of what the absolute truth of the matter is. Truth is sacrificed.

Another element in this persisting predicament is a slow erosion of integrity when the ideal is put before us, causing us to rely on our human resources to live out that ideal. If this text is true, along with this loss of integrity comes a loss of life. I would like to give Luke credit for recognizing a good story. What happens, even in terms of theology, is not that everybody who begins to cheat, or everyone who tries to give an appearance higher than one's actual performance, will immediately fall dead. But if you speed it up, the beginning of death is the point of a loss of integrity.

Just as I stopped to identify the ideal arrangement, would you agree that not only the rich but also the poor and middle-class—all of us—are victims of this persisting predicament? We long to appear in the best light but are not always willing to pay the price for the appearance? Thus a slow erosion of truth and a steady loss of integrity take place when our security is under consideration. Isn't that usually the way it is?

Living in the Tension with Integrity

So where does our text leave us? After much prayer about this, I think I hear a call to a new level of commitment. I've considered the ideal arrangements, have acknowledged the persisting predicament, and think I am beginning to experience an emerging commitment. When Peter in essence said, "Ananias, why did you think you could pull this off on the Spirit? Didn't you know the land was your own, and that nobody mandated that you had to give it up, and even after you sold it, the price that you got was yours. You could have said, 'I'm only able to offer this part.'" Even Peter gives us a clue as to what we can do despite our persisting predicament.

Christian faith always has been a faith that places one in a state of tension between the ideal arrangement and the persisting human proclivities. To live a Christian life is to live in the midst of that tension.

Philanthropy often functions out of a kind of abdication of hopefulness regarding the biblical idea. To be a Christian is to know what is in the mind of God, as our Scriptures would reveal, and to know what is in our hearts from day to day—and to refuse to break the tension either by a reduction of the vision or by a denial of the continuing human proclivity to appear to be more than we are. It is learning to tell the truth about the tension. It is the responsibility of every Christian to learn to live with integrity.

This story calls us to learn to live in the tension with integrity. We don't have to lie, pretend, or try to keep up with others. But we need to learn to live, give, and share. Our willingness to sacrifice for the good of the community gives evidence that the resurrected Lord has taken residence in our hearts.

We cannot rest completely until we are involved in a sanctifying process by which our increasing capacity to trust leads to an increased capacity to give and to support the vision of the kingdom as it has been articulated in the prophetic tradition as well as the New Testament tradition. We must learn to live in this tension and cultivate a mature sense of community where we are able daily to rise above that debilitating impact of human insecurity as we increase our trust in the power of God.

From this text, I hear a word for those of us who are involved in development, in stewardship commissions, and in making resources available for our institutions. Our underlying responsibility is to move in such a way that from where we stand, we support the development of community in which the sayings and deeds of Jesus are remembered and transmitted. That is to say, the life, the teachings, the deeds, the death, the resurrection, and the ascension of Jesus constitute the source of our mandate.

Our notion of how the world ought to be shaped—politically, socially, and economically—is derived from looking at the way Jesus did it. We look at what he said; we consider how he remembered the prophetic tradition of which he was a part. We do not form our understanding of how the world should be shaped from the current social or political arrangement. We, like the New Testament community, should live and learn what Jesus said and take it seriously.

In my church, they used to insist that deacons be spiritually mature and that trustees have clear heads. It seems now, in the light of this story, that you are the ones for whom we should petition a fresh outpouring of the Holy Spirit. You need to embody not a spirituality that lends you to mechanisms of money management but a spirituality that calls you to take seriously the ideals of the faith, a spirituality that sustains your longing to walk in the clear light of Christian compassion and sacrifice.

Father Divine used to say that he was not only to preach the gospel but to "tangibilitate" the gospel. Your jobs are to "tangibilitate" the vision of the ideal arrangement as you live in tension.

Finally, our challenge is to reach the kind of maturity where, instead of intimidating people and trying to force them to conform to a pattern, we cultivate in our communities a sense of respect so that people are free to work through their tension under the guidance of the Spirit and the encouragement and challenge of loving brothers and sisters.

Preaching the gospel is one of the ways we can teach people to live in the tension with integrity. I am convinced that if each of us does his or her part, the maturity of the community will begin to spread the ideal of which we speak. Our personal witness is the corroborating evidence necessary to drive the message home.

So don't be afraid of the tension, and don't be afraid to challenge people to give. Don't be timid about urging persons to aspire to the gospel ideal. Tell them of the gifts of the Spirit, which have been provided to help us move from death to life. And if you help people transcend their selfishness and insecurity so that they become gratefully generous, be assured that it will be entered in your heavenly record as "an act of charity toward the rich."

All Scripture quotations in this sermon are from the Revised Standard Version of the Bible unless otherwise noted.

In Need of a Miracle

Jeremiah A. Wright, Jr.

Then the LORD said to Elijah, "Now go to the town of Zarephath, near Sidon, and stay there. I have commanded a widow who lives there to feed you." So Elijah went to Zarephath, and as he came to the town gate, he saw a widow gathering firewood. "Please bring me a drink of water," he said to her. And as she was going to get it, he called out, "And please bring me some bread, too."

She answered, "By the living LORD your God I swear that I don't have any bread. All I have is a handful of flour in a bowl and a bit of olive oil in a jar. I came here to gather some firewood to take back home and prepare what little I have for my son and me. That will be our last meal, and then we will starve to death."

"Don't worry," Elijah said to her. "Go on and prepare your meal. But first make a small loaf from what you have and bring it to me, and then prepare the rest for you and your son. For this is what the LORD, the God of Israel, says: 'The bowl will not run out of flour or the jar run out of oil before the day that I, the LORD, send rain.'"

The widow went and did as Elijah had told her, and all of them had enough food for many days. As the LORD had promised through Elijah, the bowl did not run out of flour nor did the jar run out of oil.

Some time later the widow's son got sick; he got worse and worse, and finally he died. She said to Elijah, "Man of God, why did you do this to me? Did you come here to remind God of my sins and so cause my son's death?"

"Give the boy to me," Elijah said. He took the boy from her arms, carried him upstairs to the room where he was staying, and laid him on the bed. Then he prayed aloud, "O LORD my God, why have you done such a terrible thing to this widow? She has been kind enough

---

Jeremiah A. Wright, Jr., serves as senior pastor of Trinity United Church of Christ, Chicago, Illinois. He is professor and mentor for Wright/Kunjufu Fellows United Theological Seminary, Dayton, Ohio. He has been actively involved in many civic and religious organizations, has composed several hymns, and frequently preaches at churches throughout the country.

to take care of me, and now you kill her son!" Then Elijah stretched himself out on the boy three times and prayed, "O LORD my God, restore this child to life!" The LORD answered Elijah's prayer; the child started breathing again and revived.

Elijah took the boy back downstairs to his mother and said to her, "Look, your son is alive!"

She answered, "Now I know that you are a man of God and that the LORD really speaks through you!" (I Kings 17:8-24)

This woman sounds like a lot of women who have sat in my office and women who sit in our midst week after week. She is a single parent trying to raise a child. She has the double burden of trying to raise a "manchild" all by herself . . . a momma much like your momma and many of our mommas: no money, no man, and in a no-win situation! No way to feed herself, no way to feed her son. Just doing what my grandma used to call "making do."

It has always been amazing to me how country folk can take next to nothing and "make do." My daddy did the cooking at our house, and Daddy could take nothing and make a feast. He'd make you "filled up" and make you feel like you had just been to a banquet. And sometimes he had just about the same ingredients as this woman out in the country near Sidon—a hand full of flour and a little oil.

Daddy would take a little bit of flour and put in the lima beans to make the consistency thicker—make it stick to your bones—and make you feel like you had eaten a lot more than you actually had. A handful of flour and "make do."

Other times Daddy would take leftover potatoes and mash them up, then take a handful of flour, some seasoning, sometimes a little onion, and make potato cakes. He'd put them in the frying pan with a little bit of oil and make you think you had a seven-course meal. A handful of flour and "make do."

Daddy would take flour and make biscuits—not from the supermarket but from scratch! On the highfalutin days, we'd put butter on the biscuits and pour syrup or Karo or black strap molasses. You were sure 'nuff living high on the hog when you got Log Cabin or that fast-moving stuff. We used the syrup that was slower than Heinz coming out of that bottle. Syrup and biscuits—a meal fit for a king!

On the "get down" days when we couldn't afford syrup, Daddy would take a handful of flour and a little bit of oil and make gravy for the biscuits. He'd put the flour in after the oil had gotten hot and stir until it got thick and brown—and we've have gravy running all down the biscuits and all over the plate. A handful of flour and a little bit of oil. "Making do."

Well, this woman in 1 Kings 17 was doing just that—making do with a handful of flour and a little bit of olive oil in a jar. She went to get what my people used to call "kinglin' wood" to make a fire and cook . . . either some hot-water stovetop bread or some gravy with that. Times were hard for this single parent. Not only was she broke, but there was also a recession. The brook dried up and the food ran out. Not only didn't she know where her next meal was coming from; not only was she having difficulty providing for her child . . .

Have you ever had somebody depending on you, looking to you for help, looking to you for sustenance? Looking to you for something to eat, and you didn't have any help to give? It is an awful feeling. You talk about being helpless and hopeless. Have you ever heard a baby cry itself to sleep hungry? It's a different sound. It is an *awful* sound. It is a sound that haunts you way over in the daytime. Normally when the baby cries, we just get up and give it a bottle or give it a breast and put it back to sleep. But it is a different story when there is no milk either in the bottle or in the breast. No water. No food. No lights. No heat. No surplus. No mate. Nowhere to turn; and the shrieks of the little one looking up at you with trusting eyes, wondering why you won't do something about the pain in its belly. Those shrieks will give you nightmares in the daytime.

This woman was down to her last meal. Broke and burdened. Defeated and depressed. Wondering what in the world she was supposed to do next. Have you ever done all you can do, and it's still not good enough? When you have done all you can do, it makes you wonder, what *do* I do next? What *can* I do next? What *should* I do next? What *is* there to do? This woman was in need of a miracle. She was where some of us are right now: in need of a miracle.

As we worship this Sunday, I know three different members and three different health crises that are in need of a miracle. One member lies in a coma. The EEG says that there is no hope. That member is in need of a miracle. Another member has a blood disorder and the doctors haven't figured out yet what it is or what to do. Is it leukemia? Is it sickle cell anemia? Is it mononucleosis? Is it leukocytosis? Is it plasma deficiency? Is it hemoflagelia? Doctors don't know. The hematologist doesn't know. The member is in need of a miracle. Yet another member faces a surgeon's scalpel and the possibility that the tissue to be removed is cancerous. All are members in need of a miracle.

We have unemployed members, members who thought that they would be out of work only for a little while—a couple of weeks, or a month at the most. Things begin to look desperate when that "month" turns into six months, eight months, and over a year. These are people in need of a miracle.

There are families thrown into crisis as tempers flare and ugly words fly. Objects are thrown, fits are thrown. Instead of making appointments at the counselor's office, folks are making appointments at the lawyer's office— stubborn people who say they don't need any help, but their marriage is going to hell in a handbasket. Somebody is in need of a miracle.

We need what I call a "new family order," a *new* black family where never again does a black man hit a black woman! Men, have you ever considered the psychological games we play when it comes to our women? We make all kinds of rationalizations as to why we should use physical violence rather than the tough work of talking out our problems and working through difficult situations. Why does a brother hit a sister? Judge R. Eugene Pincham says it is because "he can't be what he ain't seen!" And if a brother hasn't seen a black man who is tough in the world and tender with his woman, taut in the boardroom and tender in the bedroom, taut with his foes and tender with his family—if he's not seen it, he can't be it. You can't be what you can't see. That brother whose options are limited because his perspective is limited not only needs help; that brother is in need of a miracle. Somebody is in need of a miracle.

Others are in the process of destroying that which means the most to them in the whole wide world. They don't know why. They cannot stop what it is they are doing. They want to but they can't. They got a case of what my momma used to call the "can't-help-its." Somebody is in need of a miracle.

Somebody else, like the woman in our text, is at the end of her resources, and there is no relief in sight, no change in the situation, no dramatic turnaround in the way things are going. Maybe you can relate. You have prayed and prayed and prayed, and you are just about prayed out. You are in need of a miracle.

Somebody at worship in God's sanctuary is down on himself. You've got a habit, and the habit has got you. You've tried twenty-nine-day inpatient programs, and you've slipped and fallen again. You've tried AA and NA and talking to yourself, and nothing's working! You are right back where you woke up the first day in the pigpen and came to yourself. You've tried, and you've tried, and you've tried, and you *still* keep on messing up. You are in need of a miracle.

Somebody's finances are in shambles. Oh, you are looking good here this morning. Fact is you look good most Sundays. But you ain't got a quarter in savings, and you are up to your gazoo in debt. The credit cards and plastic have gotten you so far behind the eight ball that you can't even begin to hope to see daylight. You owe *everybody* and you're late on *everything.* Tithing sounds like a cuss word to you now because you don't have enough to make it from payday to payday. (Just a little footnote here: You don't tithe with "what you've got left." You give God God's part *first* and watch what a difference that makes! End of footnote.) You can't start doing that now, however, because you are one step away from Chapter 13—though you're looking so good in your "Sunday-go-to-meetings." Somebody is in need of a miracle.

Others—oh, you see them smiling every week on the outside—are hurting like hell on the inside, and the pain will not go away. There is nobody who really understands. Nobody who will really listen without coming out of that phony holy bag on them. "Oh, honey, you just pray about it now. I know exactly what you are going through." No you don't! So they have given up trying to find authentic friendship, and everything they do is on the surface and superficial level because deep down inside they are dying, slowly dying, and need to talk to somebody; but nobody cares about them enough to genuinely listen!

Do you have any idea what it is like to try to tell others what is really inside you? You feel it way down in your gut, and they cut you off? Or they try to hit on you? You are trying to get some understanding, and they are trying to get some jones? Do you know what that is like? You are grappling with life-and-death issues, and they are talking about something that they saw on "Oprah Winfrey" or "All My Children." You are talking about your life, and they are talking about how attractive you are! You are talking about kids dying for no reason, and they are talking some pop theology that is more pap than pop, more shadow than substance; they never do hear what you are saying. So you give up. Oh, let me tell you! You see these people every week smiling and praising God on the outside, but on the inside they are hurting and asking God why. Why? Somebody is in need of a miracle this morning.

You have done all you can do, like this woman, and you can't do anymore. You just don't have the energy or the will. Well, let me tell you two things this Sunday, and then I'll be through.

If you are in need of a miracle and are in the Lord's will, number one, you are in good company. Look at the company you keep! Abraham up on the mountain, a knife in his hand, a knot in his throat, a son on the altar, and questions in his mind. Abraham was in need of a miracle.

Look at the company you keep! Moses down at the Red Sea, an angry ocean in front of him, Pharaoh's army in back of him, impassable mountains on each side of him, and an impossible situation surrounding him. Moses was in need of a miracle.

Look at the company you keep! Joshua standing outside the walls of Jericho with nothing but a ram's horn in his hands. Joshua was in need of a miracle.

Turn to your neighbor and say: "I'm in good company!"

Look at the company you keep! Hannah with no children. A barren womb mocking her and a bitter woman making fun of her. Hannah was in need of a miracle.

Look at the company you keep! Deborah at Mount Tabor facing Sisera's whole army. Deborah was in need of a miracle.

Look at the company you keep! Ruth with no man and no money. No way of making it and no way of getting back home. Ruth was in need of a miracle.

Turn to the neighbor sitting on the other side of you and say: "I am in good company!"

Look at the company you keep! David looking at Goliath with only a slingshot and five smooth stones. Nelson Mandela in prison for twenty-seven years for something he didn't do! Nzinga facing the entire Portuguese army with nothing but a few loyal troops and a whole lot of faith! Rosa Parks facing the

Birmingham police with nothing but some tired feet and a made-up mind! If you need a miracle, you are in good company.

Say it again: "I am in good company!" That is number one.

Now, number two: Not only are you in good company; you are also in good hands! Facing whatever it is you are facing that is impossible in your life, I've got some news for you: you're in good hands.

You are in good hands first of all because God knows what you need. You see, we get so focused in on the problem that we often forget the One who provides. Look at verse seven. We see a recessional situation. The brook dried up. The job ran out. The money dried up. The patience ran out. The problem got worse. The stage is set for an awful ending.

And then in verse twelve, we hear the cry of despair and see our *own* handwriting on the wall. All I have is a handful of flour and a little bit of oil. All I have is a life of broken dreams and broken promises. All I have is a body that used to be healthy but now is all used up. All I have is a boy to raise and a daddy who don't give a damn. All I have is an abusive spouse and a loveless marriage. All I have is bills to pay and no way to pay them. All I have is a habit I can't break and a relationship I can't take! All I have is a shell of an existence and nobody to share the *real* me with! All I have is a handful of flour, and what little I do have is for my son and me. This is going to be our last meal, and then we are going to starve to death!

But when we look at verse seven and verse twelve, we tend to miss verse eight. In verse eight God has got this woman's address. God knows exactly where she lives. God knows precisely what she's got and what she is going through. And God knows just what she needs. God knows your address, you zip code, your phone number, your beeper number, and your private number. God knows exactly where you live, precisely what you are going through, and just what it is you need. You are in good hands because God knows exactly what you need. Say: "I'm in good hands!"

You are in good hands, second of all, because God has already made a way. What the woman didn't know was that God had already made a way; and what you and I need to remember when we are in need of a miracle is that God has already made a way. We might not see it right now. In fact, we might be looking right at it and not see it because sometimes God sends a miracle in the ordinary. Like in a bowl or in a jar. Ordinary! A handful of flour and a little bit of oil. Ordinary! We will miss the miracle God is working in the ordinary because we are too busy looking for the extraordinary. You might not be able to see it, but look again. God has already made a way! You are in good hands! Say it one more time: "I am in good hands! I am in good company!"

You are in good hands not only because God knows what you need, not only because God has already made a way, but ultimately because God is still working even when you can't see *how* God is working. That woman must have kept going back to that bowl and looking at it, and looking at it, and looking at it. Then she would look around and see if anybody else was looking. And I am sure that she was giving it the third degree and talking to herself, trying to figure out how God was doing that. Trying to see how in the world the bowl kept filling up, and kept filling up, and kept filling up! She would no doubt be doing the same thing you and I would be doing if we experienced that kind of miracle in our lives! We would be trying to see *what* God was doing and *how* God was doing it!

Thank God that the way God works is completely independent of what you can see, what you can understand, and how you are going to be able to figure it out. God works regardless of your ability or inability to fathom, or your skill at being able to piece together all the ways that it might be possible for God to do that.

You can't see *how* God is doing what God is doing, but that's how the Lord works! He is still working even when you can't see him or what he is doing! He is still working even when you don't understand how he is working. That's how the Lord works. God had taken care of the situation long before this widow got down to her last handful!

As we say in our tradition: "He may not come when you want him!" Black folks right now want answers to their problems. We want the Lord to come now. He may not come when you want him. Family members who are sick in body and sick in mind and sick in spirit, they want the Lord to come right now; but he may not come when you want him. Single parents want some help now. We want the Lord to come now; but he may not come when you want him. When your marriage is in a mess and pain is in your heart and stubbornness hurts, you want some help right now! But he may not come when you want him! When you have more month left than you've got money left, you want the Lord now! But he may not come when you want him.

The saying does not stop there, though. It goes on to say: "Oh, but he's fixing it right now." I'm glad to know that's how the Lord works! That's just like God!

If you are in need of a miracle, remember that the God we serve is a God who supplies every need and who meets us at the point of need. We are in good company, and we are in good hands. God knows what we need. God has already made a way, and God is working on the problem from the other side even when we cannot see how God is working or understand the ways in which God works! As Thomas Dorsey urges us to remember, when we are in need of a miracle, "The Lord will make a way, somehow!"

All Scripture quotations in this sermon are from the Good News Bible unless otherwise noted.

Kids for the Kingdom

Robert G. Murray

"Suffer the little children to come unto me, and forbid them not; for of such is the kingdom of God." (Mark 10:14)

"The kingdom of God!" "The kingdom of God!" *"The kingdom of God!"* The Scriptures declare that this was the heart of the message and ministry of our Lord and Savior Jesus Christ. Mark recorded that once Jesus arrived in Galilee, this became his proclamation: "The time is fulfilled, and the kingdom of God is at hand; repent ye, and believe the gospel" (Mark 1:15). The kingdom was an imperative of his teachings. The Lord spoke of the high priority of the kingdom of God when he addressed that audience on the mountain and said to them, "But seek ye first the kingdom of God, and his righteousness, and all these things shall be added unto you" (Matthew 6:33). In his famous Beatitudes, he used this idea of the kingdom of God (or the kingdom of heaven) several times.

He not only taught us about the kingdom of God; he also taught us to pray for it. In the prayer that we call the Lord's Prayer, the concept of the kingdom is mentioned twice: once to usher it in—"thy Kingdom come" (Matthew 6:10)—and the other time to confirm its existence and its owner—"for thine is the kingdom" (Matthew 6:13).

The kingdom is often viewed as a utopia. It certainly requires a radical change for entrance and residency. In the story of Nicodemus, whom Jesus converted in Jerusalem's darkness, Jesus spoke of the true requirements for the kingdom: "Except a man be born again, he cannot see the kingdom of God" (John

Robert G. Murray is pastor of the First Baptist Church, Norfolk, Virginia. He is president of the Norfolk Coalition for Quality Public Education and secretary of the Lott Carey Foreign Mission Convention. He has served as adjunct professor at Virginia Commonwealth University in the Departments of Afro-American Studies and Religious Studies and is a freelance columnist for the *Journal and Guide* weekly newspaper.

3:3). On another occasion, Jesus expounded on the difficulty of entering the kingdom of heaven for those who thought that they had easy access into the kingdom based on their heritage and riches. Jesus shocked them with this hard and harsh statement: "It is easier for a camel to go through the eye of a needle than for a rich man to enter into the kingdom of God" (Matthew 19:24). You can be certain also that the Lord must have shattered the idealistic view that some people had of the kingdom of God overflowing with milk and honey. Paul did not make it any better for those wishful and theological pleasure-seekers when he said, "The kingdom of God is not meat and drink; but righteousness, and peace, and joy in the Holy Ghost" (Romans 14:17).

Some people saw it as being far off, yet Jesus expressed in his preaching and teaching its immediacy. He said, "The kingdom of God is come upon you" (Luke 11:20), and "The kingdom of God is within you" (Luke 17:21). Perhaps we need to know that it is both now and yet to come, and since it is the Lord's kingdom, it is always wherever he is, where he rules and reigns in our lives.

It was Jesus' purpose to proclaim the ideal for men, women, boys, and girls: to become residents of the kingdom of God. This pronouncement was primarily one that identified Jesus as the Savior to a world that needed his saving grace. However, his call to persons to follow him often meant great sacrifices because he himself had given up so much for the sake of the kingdom. On one occasion, he told some would-be disciples that "foxes have holes, and birds of the air have nests, but the Son of man hath no where to lay his head" (Luke 9:58). Pursuing the kingdom requires commitment and determination: "No man," said the Lord, "having put his hand to the plow, and looking back, is fit for the kingdom of God" (Luke 9:62).

Along with this imperative about the kingdom of God, Jesus also taught about stewardship, for the notions of sacrifice and commitment are important to kingdom living. Our Lord and Savior was not only teaching the people about the eternal life aspects of the kingdom; on numerous occasions he wanted them to see that the kingdom required a life of devotion and dedication. The Lord, being a master picture-painter, often used parables to tell the story of the kingdom of God, and many of these stories told of how his kingdom was "likened onto" those who were good stewards of the possessions of God. He told the parable of the ten virgins (Matthew 25:1-13), where the resources of oil and time were crucial, and the sequel to this parable, the parable of the talents (Matthew 25:14-30), where both eternal and temporal rewards can be based on our attitudes toward productivity. Most of the time the Lord used parables as a means of giving a stewardship message concerning the kingdom of God.

Once, however, he used a live example to illustrate the importance of his kingdom and how we must be responsible to it. He did not use the examples around him—mustard seeds or leaven, fig trees or plowed fields, oil lamps or talents. Instead, the Lord took children up in his arms with tender care and blessed them and said, ". . . of such is the kingdom of God" (Mark 10:14). There is no doubt that when he spoke these words he was speaking about the nature of the kingdom of God. Here again is that radical and surprising approach that Jesus often took: the kingdom is for those who have childlike ways as opposed to the hard and fixed attitudes of many adults. Kids are certainly good kingdom candidates, and they also have the potential to be good stewards for the Lord.

In his commentary *The Gospel of Mark,* Dr. William Barclay outlined why the Lord preferred childlike attitudes for his kingdom.[1] Let me expound upon Barclay's ideas:

Children have **humility.** They are not concerned with prominence, publicity, place, pride, or prestige. Children do not know their own importance, which makes them malleable for the importance of God in their lives. They have not learned how to be self-centered, thus they can become more Christ-centered.

Children are **obedient.** Even the best children will misbehave, but they will usually respond to those who correct them or even try to do what's right in order to avoid punishment. But even more so, children will be obedient as an act of love, because they don't want to hurt their loved ones. Thus children can be excellent stewards. Children can learn about tithing as an act of law and love, and when they are taught, they will not depart from your teachings (Proverbs 22:6).

Children are **trusting.** Perhaps this is the one reason why a childlike attitude is essential for the kingdom. Children will trust without reservation. Someone once said that the greatest compliment ever paid him was when a little boy came up to him, a complete stranger, and asked him to tie his shoelace! It is this attitude that will take the risk to do things when it seems uncommon and unconventional. It is this attitude of trust that will put our world back into order, return our neighborhoods and communities back to peaceful and friendly places in which to live, and make our homes places of joy and love.

It is these characteristics of children that Jesus was referring to when he spoke of the kingdom of God. Now it is our challenge for today and into the next century to see the importance of children, youth, and young adults in the kingdom of God. It is imperative that this generation which has been labeled "the lost generation" be found, and that we find a place for them in our churches and communities. As stewards of God, we have a great challenge to make "kids for the kingdom." Jesus said that "of such is the kingdom of God." If they were important to him, then should we not also see them as important?

This passage of Scripture demonstrated how important children are to the Lord, and certainly how he used them as a model of the behavioral pattern he's looking for in his kingdom. It's a text that also tells us that parents are most significant in preparing youth for the kingdom of God. The passage says, "And they brought young children to him, that he should touch them." This is the beginning of stewardship. This is human creation. This is where God entrusted his most important commodity, human life, into human hands. This is where *real responsibility* begins as parents bring forth a life and spend their lives nurturing their children. (As so many of you parents know, you never stop being a parent.)

This is also accountability, for what our children become has a lot to do with the type of environment we create for them. The sad statistics of today are proof of this. Children who are abused often will become child abusers; those who grow up in the midst of alcohol and drug addiction may very well become alcoholics and drug addicts or marry someone who is addicted. On the other hand, when children are in an atmosphere of love and caring, then they in turn are more able to provide for their children. This we can say for certain: parents have a tremendous responsibility in shaping and sharpening "kids for the kingdom."

It is significant to note that in this Bible story these parents brought their children to Jesus. One of the customs of that time and region was to bring children to meet and be blessed by a renowned rabbi, and certainly Jesus was one of the most famous. These parents wanted their children to be exposed to the information and inspiration that would come from a great teacher. It must be said that the problems we have today and will face in the future are due largely to the fact that we have abandoned some of those old values!

There was a time when our parents did as their parents did and took their children to Jesus, to the place where they could learn about Jesus, namely, the church. Some of us remember well the Saturday night rituals—the baths, the clothes being put out, and the dinner being prepared—because you didn't cook on Sunday, and you didn't eat either, if you did not go to church! It was totally a family affair. That next morning, which was Sunday, our legs and faces would be greased to a shine to match the shoes that were shined, our ties were straightened and petticoats adjusted so that the ruffles would show, and it was off to church we'd go. You were brought! You were not dropped off! You were brought, and your parents stayed there with you.

There is a need to return to these values of yesterday, when we maintained and sustained family values and spent time with one another. It is important for parents, if they want to bring out the greatest potential in their children, to spend more time home with them instilling spiritual values in them in the midst of a valueless society.

In an article in *Essence* magazine, December 1991, entitled "Parenting: The Spiritual Connection," Joy Duckett Cain stated that children have the capacity to learn about God, but they must be taught in a way they can understand. She further stated that through the experience of church involvement, parents can help their children to develop their own spiritual ties, which will help them in today's society. "It is important that children feel connected with God for a variety of reasons: the connection increases self-confidence, gives a sense of security and well-being and instills a belief in the goodness of others. Most of all, by having this link and knowing that they are not alone, children will be better able to handle the disappointments and hard knocks that will surely come their way."[2]

Yes, parents have the moral responsibility of preparing their children for the future, and, even more so, we all have the responsibility of seeing these young people as potential citizens in God's kingdom, citizens who can make a positive contribution. This is the way we were brought up in the "old African village" system where a child was not born to one set of parents but to the entire community.

I had neighbors, teachers, and members of my church family who saw my potential and abilities long before I knew how to spell the word *potential.* We have to see once again the importance of our existence. The Akan tribe said it best: "I am because you are and you are because I am." In other words, where there are no responsible parents, then other members of the family need to step forth and become the mother and father. Neighbors and friends need to step forth and take up the slack, and Lord knows, the church family needs to design ways to embrace the youth of today following the theme "Each one reach one and teach one."

All of us must see ourselves with parenting responsibilities because we cannot afford to lose our children. *All* of them have so much potential and ability. Recently I read an article that brought home to me the potential of our young people today. The article was about some youth in the inner-city area of our nation's capital who, without a special scholarship program, would not be able to attend college. Each student had to write an essay that explained how something he or she learned in school had affected their lives. The essay of one young person was on how he had huddled under a tree with other people during a violent thunderstorm and how his knowledge of science saved his life:

I began to correlate it scientifically.... The multitude of people standing under the tree would generate a mass of electrons that might attract electrical charges in a storm cloud and complete a very large and potentially lethal circuit. I did what any other person would do—I ran. And then I heard the crack of lightning that struck the tree, killing 15-year-old Noah Eig and injuring 10 others.[3]

This must have been a traumatic experience for this African American child, who was able to go back to a physics class and recall theories on electricity and thus quickly think that he needed to run for his life. But I wondered, too, what life would have been like for him if some parent had not pushed him to study, if some teachers had not worked with his potential, and if some other persons had not encouraged him along the way. He is now on his way to the University of Maryland on a full scholarship. He is studying to be an electrical engineer (quite appropriate, I think). As parents and surrogate parents, we need to see the potential in every child God has given us. This young man and other young men and women are children of the King, and we have a moral responsibility to try to produce, promote, and then preserve them!

Certainly it is important that parents bring their children to the Lord, that we see them as blessings from God, and that we take these blessings of God to make them all that God would have them to be. But there is one problem. This Scripture passage painfully shows that there was then, and there is now, a problem with how the church and the society view children.

The Lord was on his way to Calvary. He no doubt could hear the death knell. He could feel the spikes vibrating in his hands and feet. He could taste the droplets of blood flowing past his lips from the crown of thorns on his head. He had an appointment with destiny, a cross to bear, a world to save. Time was of the essence; *yet he took time to pick up the little children in his arms* and said to all who heard him, ". . . of such is the kingdom of God." This famous statement on the relationship of the kingdom of God to having a childlike attitude was based also on the rebuke and the rejection of his disciples toward these children and their parents. Jesus had to tell his disciples to not hinder the children to come to him.

It must be said that these disciples were well intentioned. They thought that they were protecting their Lord, trying to prevent the invasion of his privacy. They were keeping these kids out of his path and life. Yet, the truth of the matter was that this was rejection and negligence regarding children on the part of this early nucleus of the church. Those kids then, as now, needed to be ministered to and to be brought to the Lord.

The problem with our youth today is not drugs; they're only a symptom. The trouble with our young people today is not violence and crime; those are only the effects from a far greater cause. Our youth do not produce or distribute drugs or guns, yet they are the victims of them. The problem that they suffer from the most is rejection and alienation. We speak of them as a "lost generation."

The Los Angeles riots in April 1992, which I prefer to call the "L.A. Revolution," revealed just how much our nation had abandoned our youth and those who are poor and disinherited. Young people expressed their despair and hopelessness as they went on a rampage to destroy a city; but their actions got our attention and woke up a nation that had been lulled by the false idea of some that "all is well." During the L.A. incident a story was recalled about the 1965 Watts riot. At that time Dr. Martin Luther King, Jr., went to Watts and asked a jubilant crowd of young men and women the question, "How can you say you won when 34 Negroes are dead, your community is destroyed, and whites are using the riots as an excuse for inaction?" Dr. King recalled their response: "We won because we made them pay attention to us."[4]

The point I want to make is that people—and especially children—realize that if they want to get some attention, all they have to do is "act out." Matter of fact, I had an uncle who said to me that if we give kids candy to shut them up when they are crying, we only teach them that if they make noise, they will get some candy!

Our society is practically pushing our children down the path of problems and helping them to travel the road of trouble. Our school systems have done their share to increase the dropout rates; our parks and recreation programs have put youth out in the streets; and our social services have helped to tear down the family structure with their welfare programs. Thus, when people are rejected and neglected, they will soon fight back. They will do things to get attention. They will turn to negative behaviors such as drugs, crime, teenage pregnancies, and so on. The numbers are astronomical and are outdated each year. We can see the problem. We know that there is a problem, yet we don't want to admit that we ourselves are the problem!

Jesus responded to these "would-do-good" brethren: "Suffer the little children to come unto me, and forbid them not; for of such is the kingdom of God." He was telling them not to let the children get away. Do not turn them away, do not reject them or neglect them. Bring them to me. What he said then is important for us to heed right now!

A revealing study by C. Eric Lincoln and Laurence H. Mamiya, *The Black Church in the African American Experience,* indicated that the church is losing its youth and young adults at a rapid rate.[5] Some of it is due to the lack of identifying a relevant ministry for them and understanding the pressures and challenges that young people are experiencing today. Some of it is a result of taking them for granted and focusing our attention on the base of givers who can do more for the church's finance, namely adults. Some of it is thinking that buildings and management are more important than providing a place for loud and unruly children, who have a real need to be loved and disciplined. The church has, in some cases, abandoned our children and has failed to minister to them. The one lesson that we can learn from Jesus in this text is that he got the youth involved. On another occasion he put them at the center of his ministry (Mark 9:35-37).

We cannot afford to lose our children, but we are doing just that whenever we leave them out. When we exclude them from the ministries of our churches, we provide the opportunities for the drug dealers, the cults, and the occult. When we fail to challenge them with revelation and relevance, then the "parachurches" and "Afrocentric sects," both spiritual and secular, will compete against us and win! They are doing so because they are involving our black youth. The Black Muslims are taking young men who have been hardened criminals and getting them involved in their program. We must create a place where youth can feel that their church is "user friendly" and create an alternative, especially for those who grow up in hostile environments where they cannot find love and care. We must help them find refuge in the time of storm. If we leave them alone or exclude them, the church will become part of the problem rather than part of the solution.

We need to understand that *having ministries that identify with youth and the needs of youth is good stewardship!* There is an old adage that says, "An idle mind is the devil's workshop." Parents ask of children, especially when they do not hear any noise, "What's going on?" "What are you doing?" They know that silence means you might be up to something. Or, they might ask that classic question if they know you are not doing anything: "Why don't you do something constructive?" Because parents old and new know that if children do not have anything *con*structive to do, they might do something *de*structive—and get attention the wrong way.

Kids need to be involved! They need to have something to do. When they have nothing to do, they will get bored. And when they get bored, they will get in trouble! But the challenge for us today and into the next century is how to get youth involved and combat their boredom with innovative ministries.

Jawanza Kunjufu, in his book *Motivating and Preparing Black Youth to Work,* offers an excellent idea and a principle that may help us solve this problem. Kunjufu speaks about an African perspective on dealing with boredom and the lack of youth involvement. He says that "boredom does not come from outside in but the inside out."[6] He explores an African concept called "inner attainment," in which there is no separation between performance and audience; when the drummers play, all the people dance. The European variant is called "entertainment," best illustrated at the opera where there is not only a distinctive separation, but the audience only claps at designated intervals.[7] In other words, you can enjoy something even more when you are a part of it, when you are involved in the planning of it, when you can make a contribution to it, and when you enjoy what you are doing.

Jesus did not entertain the children; instead, he got them involved. He used "inner attainment"! He included the children in his agenda, and he made them a part of his itinerary. He gave them room in his life and made them subjects in his curriculum. But even more than that, he made them residents of his kingdom. We cannot afford to count anyone out—and certainly not our youth. Our kids are too important. We have got to get them so involved that they will not have time for drugs, time for crime, time for unwanted pregnancies, time to be a school dropout, not even time to waste time! If we get them involved, as Jesus did, then they may understand what the slaves were singing about:

> Keep so busy working for my Jesus,
> Keep so busy working for my Lord,
> Keep so busy working for my Master,
> Ain't got time to die!

A beautiful picture was painted as Jesus picked up the children in his arms and blessed them. There could be no doubt that he had included them by this gesture of love. But he also blessed them. As he faced his own destiny, he knew what kind of future they had to face, and he blessed them. How many times have we faced life's many vicissitudes with greater certainty because we were blessed by the Lord! Our children need to know that they are blessed by the Lord.

Their future has been painted by many forecasters as very bleak. People are being discouraged from having children because of what the ecologists and economists are saying about tomorrow. Our children themselves are trying to combat their fears by packing guns in their bookbags, not books. Even those who seek a fast lifestyle in drugs and crime do not believe that they will live long; so they have adapted the Epicurean philosophy of "eat, drink, and be merry, for tomorrow you may die." Some of our youth are even flirting with sexual lifestyles with the attitude that "AIDS is unavoidable, so what do I have to lose?"

Even the job market is so questionable that despite good credentials, the employment possibilities for African American youth are always lower than the rest of the population. Tom Sine, in an article "Shifting the Church into the Future Tense," stated that "the 'Baby Busters,' the generation born since 1964, come from the most fragmented, abusive and addictive homes, and their culture reflects a growing nihilism or purposelessness."[8] Even those young people of the church, he believes, are not going to be ready to take on the leadership of the kingdom because even the church has taught them that to be blessed has to do with the accumulation of things. Perhaps our emphasis has been on the "thingdom" more than the "kingdom."

Jesus' idea of the kingdom of God was more than what we possess, but as Dr. Wendell Somerville, Executive Minister/Secretary of the Lott Carey Foreign Baptist Missions Convention, would say, "It is who possesses us!" Being blessed is more than how much I own; it is how much I know. *Blessed* is a word that is also interpreted to mean happiness. It is a blessing to know who you are and, in this world with its uncertain future, it will be a blessing to know who you are and whose you are!

The challenge of the African American Christian church is to teach our children who they are and whose they are. They need to know who they are in order to combat the negative and racist views of the society in which they must live. They need to know who they are in a world that seems purposeless and aimless. They need to know who they are in their own communities that espouse self-defeating attitudes and actions. They need to know who they are in order that they might be strong citizens of the world today and tomorrow. They need to know who they are and that they have a rich African heritage. They need to know who they are and that their parents overcame slavery and segregation. They need to know who they are and that there is nothing in this world that they cannot do because greater is he that is in them than he that is in the world!

They will be blessed if they know who they are—"kids for the kingdom"! And if they are "kids for the kingdom," then each of them can say with confidence and "blessed assurance," "I'm a child of the King!"

> My father is rich in houses and lands,
> He holdeth the wealth of the world in His hands
> Of rubies and diamonds, of silver and gold,
> His coffers are full, He has riches untold.
>
> I'm a child of the King, A child of the King
> With Jesus my Savior, I'm a Child of the King.[9]

All Scripture quotations in this sermon are from the King James Version of the Bible unless otherwise noted.

Some Time for the Mind

Jason A. Barr, Jr.

Do your best to present yourself to God as one approved, a workman who does not need to be ashamed and who correctly handles the word of truth. (2 Timothy 2:15)

With Head and Heart is the title of the autobiography of Howard Thurman. Thurman's choice of words is an apt description of wholistic Christian living. To be Christlike is more than a matter of engaging in the ephemeral pursuit of ecstatic religious experience. The life of the Christian must be characterized by more than sentimentality and the physical fervor with which we express our praises to God. If, as is popularly understood, the heart is the seat of the emotions, and if the nurture of the heart and the love of God with our hearts is the sum total of wholistic Christian living, then we are on the right track. But life in Christ and with Christ is more than a matter of the heart; it is also a matter of the mind.

The affective dimension of our Christian witness should not be understood as antithetical to our responsibility to engage our cognitive faculties in our development. The two are not mutually exclusive. The point is that often we nurture and promote the emotional side of religious experience to the exclusion of the tedious and time-consuming demands of study and inquiry.

We want to reach the heights of spiritual ecstasy. We want the preacher to make us feel good. We want to scale the mountains of religious enthusiasm. We want to sing ourselves into a holy fit. We want to shout ourselves into a transitory frenzy. We want to pray ourselves into a spiritual high. There is, to be cer-

---

Jason A. Barr, Jr., is senior pastor of the Macedonia Baptist Church in Pittsburgh, Pennsylvania. He also serves as an instructor in the Department of Africana Studies, University of Pittsburgh, and as adjunct professor at Pittsburgh Theological Seminary. He is a member of the "Committee of 100" of Renewed for Mission of the American Baptist Churches in the U.S.A.

tain, nothing wrong with any of these things. But if they become the *summum bonum* of religious experience and expression, then we have failed at fulfilling the total demands of the gospel.

There is nothing wrong with entering into an emotional rendezvous with the Holy. There is nothing wrong with feeling good—notwithstanding the fact that there are those who cast an eye of aspersion upon religious emotion. There have been many, particularly in the academic community, who have characterized the religious fervor of the black church pejoratively. Some say our praising, shouting, and singing is escapism. Others contend it is compensatory; we thus vent our pent-up aggressions and emotions in church rather than deal with the real culprits in our lives. Still others characterize the emotion of most black churches as irrational motor behavior that is more detrimental than helpful.

But no matter what the scholars say, there is nothing wrong with engaging in an emotional encounter with the living God. We are not one-dimensional creatures. We are body, mind, and soul. All dimensions of our essence need to be utilized and nurtured if we are to be whole people. We need to praise God. We need to praise God because God has been good to us. We need to praise God because the Lord has been our refuge and strength. We need to praise God because God is worthy to be praised.

And yet Christianity is also more than the collective volume of our vocal outpourings of praise on Sunday. The Christian life must also include the development of our mind and the study of God's Word. If we accept the major premise of stewardship, this fact can easily be comprehended. *The major premise of Christian stewardship is that everything we have is a gift from God.* Since each of God's human creatures has been blessed with a mind, each has a responsibility to develop and nurture his or her mind as well as all gifts given by the Creator. More specifically, the development of our minds must be done in the context of the study of God's Word.

This fact is affirmed in 2 Timothy 2:15, where Paul exhorts Timothy to "do your best to present yourself to God as one approved, a workman who does not need to be ashamed and who correctly handles the word of truth." The King James Version translates the first phrase of this verse as: "Study to show thyself approved unto God . . ." Although these words were written in the context of an older preacher giving wise counsel to a younger preacher, they nevertheless also speak to the need of all Christians to spend some time developing the mind.

There is no paucity of evidence that suggests that the typical African American church and Christian would rather nurture almost any resource from God except the mind. Floyd Massey and Samuel McKinney in their book *Church Administration in the Black Perspective* have characterized the black church as anti-intellectual.[1] A cursory perusal of the ministries of most black churches reveals that an emphasis on Sunday school, Bible study, or other programs of

Christian intellectual development is the exception rather than the rule. Most Christians are more satisfied with dynamic singing than with dynamic teaching or preaching. They prefer that which entertains to that which enlightens. If one observes most of the exhibition areas at African American national religious gatherings, it is quite apparent where we spend our time, space, and money. It has always been amusing to see the preponderance of vendors that sell clothes, jewelry, and prefabricated sermons. Relatively speaking, there is not much time, space, or money set aside for books and other resources that enhance one's intellectual development.

It is exactly this overemphasis on the finite dimensions of life that must be overcome if we are to be whole Christians. The prophet Isaiah and the apostle Peter reminded us that "the grass withers and the flowers fall, but the word of our God stands forever" (Isaiah 40:8, 1 Peter 1:24-25). When the gold and the glitter of this life has faded, God's Word will remain. When the clothes and the jewelry have been eaten by the moths and rust of this world, God's Word will remain. Our challenge is to spend some time with our minds through the study of God's Word.

The question for many at this point may be, Why should I develop my mind? Why should I engage in a disciplined study of God's Word? Why should I study the Scriptures as well as other books and resources about God and the Christian life?

There are at least four reasons to spend some time developing your mind through a disciplined study of God's Word. We spend time nurturing our mind for affirmation, stimulation, authentication, and liberation.

1. Affirmation. When we spend time developing our minds, affirmation comes from two directions: God and self. Paul tells Timothy to study and present himself such that he would be approved by God. The issue here is not that Timothy's salvation was dependent upon God's approval of Timothy's study, but that because Timothy was saved and called by God, he, in response to God's gracious acts, would prove himself worthy of what God had already done.

We do not spend time studying God's Word and equipping ourselves intellectually in order to impress God. God is not impressed with our pedantic displays of either genuine or pseudo knowledge or profundity. We cannot coerce God or cause God to act favorably toward us simply because we know "the Word" or even because we are smart. We spend time with God's Word and developing our minds not because of what we can do for God but because of what God has already done for us through Christ.

A genuine love of Christ will lead us to seek the mind of Christ. An appreciation of God's love as expressed through Christ leads us to want to know more about the God of Christ, the God in Christ, and the God that is active in the world today through the power, presence, and personality of the Holy Spirit.

When we spend time with our minds and God's Word, self-affirmation takes place. Often I have witnessed Christians who have spent much time studying and developing their skills with handling God's Word intimidate and control Christians who have not. While God's Word should never be used to intimidate or control people in such a way that one's own agenda is advanced, neither is it spiritually healthy nor virtuous for one to neglect spending time developing one's own mind.

If we took the time to diligently pursue an understanding of God's Word, we would not find ourselves forever in the position of having to submit ourselves to the intimidation, control, or even the definitions imposed on us by others. This is not to suggest that if all of us studied God's Word, conflicts and disagreements would not occur. Quite honestly, this type of discipline would probably precipitate and encourage conflict. But conflict is not as great a threat to our spiritual health as control and intimidation. We can only be controlled and intimidated if we allow others to do so.

It has been said that "knowledge is power." If this is true, then knowledge of God's Word is a tool we can use to empower ourselves in such a way that we are affirmed and freed from the control and intimidation imposed on us by others. The Christian who knows God's Word and is informed cannot be controlled by others.

2. Stimulation. Not only do we spend time with God's Word for affirmation; we also study for stimulation. Spending time with God's Word ought to stimulate one to seek to hear the voice of God in all aspects of human experience. The voice of God can be and is disclosed in the arts, literature, social sciences, natural sciences, and history. While it is true that God's self-disclosures in disciplines beyond the Scripture do not contradict God's self-disclosure in Scripture, it is equally true that God is not *fully* revealed in Scripture or any other single aspect of God's created order.

God did not cease to speak to the world when the canon was closed. God still speaks in the art of young African American artists who have begun to capture biblical themes in their work. God still speaks in the prose and poetry of Maya Angelou. God still speaks in the theologies of African Americans like James Cone and Gayraud Wilmore. God still speaks in the historical research of James Washington. God still speaks in the rhythmic rap of M. C. Hammer. God still speaks in the lives of physicians like Dr. Ben Carson.

There are those who pride themselves in the fact that they need nothing but the Bible. The Bible ought to be the standard text for the rough and difficult course of life. Yet the Bible also does to us what it has done to others like C. S. Lewis, D. Elton Trueblood, and even great African American preachers like Gardner C. Taylor. The Bible, with its true-to-life stories, sublime themes, and great doctrines, led these individuals to a grasp and appreciation of life in *all* of its dimensions. If we are to become whole Christians, we must put on the "whole armour of God" (Ephesians 6:11, KJV), which includes equipping the mind with the full measure of God's self-revelation in all aspects of life.

3. Authentication. The third reason we spend time developing our mind and studying God's Word is for authentication. Paul, as well as other New Testament writers, was acutely aware that some scattered among the elect were advancing doctrines that were not Christian. There appears in the New Testament a great concern over false teaching and false teachers. One of the reasons the writings of Paul and other New Testament writings were gathered and canonized was to aid the struggling Christian church in differentiating between true and false doctrine.

Although we are almost two thousand years removed from the concerns of the early church, we are still burdened with false teachings and false teachers. In some ways our situation is worse. Much of the false teaching we encounter today is exacerbated by the invention of the printing press and the pervasive presence of mass media, particularly television. All a person needs in our day to advance his or her own agenda worldwide, whether true or false, is money and the ability to appeal to and persuade the hungry masses. This is compounded by the fact that we are living in an age when people "will not put up with sound doctrine. Instead, to suit their own desires, they will gather around them a great number of teachers to say what their itching ears want to hear" (2 Timothy 4:3).

Now, as never before, it is imperative that every Christian spend time with God's Word in order to critically engage and refute the copious false teachings that are prevalent in our day. It is also important that each of us develops a discriminating mind. Much of what is taught today may not be false as much as an overemphasis on certain biblical axioms to the exclusion of others. Some whose teachings are questionable do not appreciate the presence of paradox in the Scriptures, particularly in the New Testament. Whatever the case, whether false teaching, partial teaching, or incorrect teaching, it is important that we Christians develop our minds to the point that we ask the critical questions and hear God's Word in its totality.

4. Liberation. The final reason to spend time developing our mind through the study of God's Word is for liberation. In Paul's letter to the Galatians, he asserts, "I am astonished that you are so quickly deserting the one who called you by the grace of Christ and are turning to a different gospel—which is really no gospel at all" (Galatians 1:6-7). Paul is addressing the Judaizers and their attempt to burden the Gentile converts with circumcision and other aspects of the law. Later in Galatians, Paul writes, "It is for freedom that Christ has set us free. Stand firm, then, and do not let yourselves be burdened again by a yoke of slavery" (5:1).

Paul's point here is that the gospel is a gospel of liberation. Although Paul was addressing slavery in the context of religious rite and ritual, it is nonetheless true that God abhors slavery in any of its manifestations. Slavery is evil whether the enslaved is shackled and chained by sin, ceremony, or culture. The gospel of our God is that there is good news. The good news is that the Christ of God has come to set the captive free. The liberation that is ours in Christ has been achieved not only for those enslaved by rite and ritual but also for those enslaved by psychological inferiority, chained by sociological stigmatization, shackled by political tyranny, or bound by any dehumanizing theology.

The liberation of African Americans from human bondage and segregation in this country cannot be divorced from the Word of God. The most strident soldiers in the struggle for our liberation have been informed, motivated, and sustained by a knowledge of the authentic Word of God. In spite of the fact that slaves were taught that slavery was the will of God, it was men like Denmark Vesey, Gabriel Prosser, and Nat Turner, who knew and studied the Word for themselves, who revolted against the status quo. It was Frederick Douglas's awareness of the authentic Word of God that caused him to question the unholy alliance between slavery and Christianity. It was the basic message of the dignity of all human beings taught in the home and church of Martin Luther King, Jr., and then honed and developed through years of study, that undergirded his quest in the struggle for freedom. Over and over again it is evident in the history of African Americans that the most vocal defenders of our freedom have been those who were intellectually equipped and biblically grounded.

The Word of God has also been the catalyst that has liberated humanity and freed God's created order to function to his glory. It was the affirming Word of God that brought order and community out of disorder and chaos. It was the liberating Word of God that motivated and inspired Moses to lead the children of Israel from Egyptian bondage to the Promised Land. It was the emancipating Word of God that lifted lifeless, dry bones from a valley of hopeless inertia. It was the inexhaustible Word of God that allowed Jesus to rebuff the insidious attacks of Satan in the wilderness. And it is the authentic and unfettered Word of God that will deliver African Americans from the plethora of "isms" and chains that keep us from achieving our full potential in Christ Jesus.

Only as we are persuaded and disciplined enough to pursue wholistic Christian development will we be true disciples of Christ. That development means the nurture of all that God has entrusted to us, which includes our mind and God's Word. If we spend time developing our mind through a study of God's Word for affirmation, stimulation, authentication, and liberation, we will discover with the psalmist that God's Word is indeed a lamp unto our feet and a light unto our path (Psalm 119:105). We will discover that our stewardship involves everything we have as a gift from God.

As we continue to allow God to finish the good work begun in us, as we struggle with the God who loves us, as we wrestle with the world God has made for us, may we be and become energized to lean on and learn of him who said, "Take my yoke upon you and *learn* from me . . ." (Matthew 11:28, italics mine).

May we affirm and join the quest of the hymn writer who wrote:

> More about Jesus would I know
> More of His grace to others show,
> More of His saving fullness see
> More of His love who died for me.
>
> More about Jesus let me learn,
> More of His Holy will discern;
> Spirit of God, my teacher be,
> Showing the things of Christ to me.
>
> More, more about Jesus,
> More, more about Jesus;
> More of His saving fullness see,
> More of His love who died for me.[2]

All Scripture quotations in this sermon are from the New International Version of the Bible unless otherwise noted.

Such As I Have

Arlee Griffin, Jr.

Now Peter and John went up together into the temple at the hour of prayer, being the ninth hour. And a certain man lame from his mother's womb was carried, whom they laid daily at the gate of the temple which is called Beautiful, to ask alms of them that entered into the temple; Who seeing Peter and John about to go into the temple asked an alms.

And Peter, fastening his eyes upon him with John, said, Look on us.

And he gave heed unto them, expecting to receive something of them.

Then Peter said, Silver and gold have I none; but such as I have give I thee: In the name of Jesus Christ of Nazareth rise up and walk.

And he took him by the right hand, and lifted him up: and immediately his feet and ankle bones received strength. And he leaping up stood, and walked, and entered with them into the temple, walking, and leaping, and praising God.

And all the people saw him walking and praising God: And they knew that it was he which sat for alms at the Beautiful gate of the temple: and they were filled with wonder and amazement at that which had happened unto him. (Acts 3:1-10)

Nobody is a nobody, despite the lyrics of that popular gospel song "I'm Just a Nobody." Everybody is God's somebody because we are made *imago dei*—in the image and likeness of God.

I find it both interesting and intriguing that of all the people who have ever lived and of all the more than five billion who currently populate Planet Earth, nobody has been or is exactly like you or me. Wow! What a wonder we are!

Arlee Griffin, Jr., serves as senior pastor of the Berean Missionary Baptist Church in Brooklyn, New York. Active on the boards of both civic and church-related organizations, he is also adjunct professor of church administration at New York Theological Seminary and has done mission work in Senegal and Gambia, West Africa.

We are wonderfully made and uniquely gifted to participate with God as cocreators in what process theologians call "the continuous eighth day of creation." In our creative partnership with God, we must never forget that life is a gift from God and that what we do with our lives is our gift back to God. From this perspective, both the gift received and the gift given become our ministry of stewardship. And as stewards of God's creation,

> Each of us is given a bag of tools
> A shapeless mass, a book of rules
> And each must make before life is gone
> A stumbling block or stepping stone.

This is how the kingdom of God will be built here on earth as it is in heaven. At Pentecost, the church was empowered by the Holy Spirit to do this unfinished business of kingdom building. And like the early church, the contemporary church must assume a posture of stewardship and practice a ministry of service in a world waiting for the church to "be and do" the church even when we thought it was not. This point is made prophetically by John Naisbitt and Patricia Aburdene in their book *Megatrends 2000,* in which they state that the turn of the century will witness a renewed interest in religion.[1] The world is waiting for Christians who understand themselves fundamentally as stewards whose faith will be a stimulus for service and not a sedative against it. In this culture saturated with the secular, stewards in their service must counter the secular with the sacred. We live in a wounded and weary world, desperately seeking an authentic, genuine life which God alone offers to all. We must not give the waiting world the false impression that God can be found only in temples that show the sacred drama on Sunday and not the daily struggles of humanity. God is not only in our high and holy places; God is also in the workplace and marketplace. God is not limited to our upper rooms; God can also be in corporate boardrooms and civil courtrooms. God is not only in our sanctuaries but also in our cemeteries of lost hopes and shattered dreams, making that which had died come alive again with resurrection power.

From our vantage point as stewards, Jesus Christ is Lord of all. We are sent forth as servants of Christ to do kingdom building. We have an order to help heal the hurts and heighten the hopes of the human family.

With this mission in mind, we can see that Peter and John are masterful models for us on their mission of mercy with the lame man at the temple gate (Acts 3:1-10). We observe in their actions three principles that should guide us as stewards in service.

First, *they made a donation.* Peter and John said to the lame man, "Silver and gold have I none; but such as I have give I thee" (Acts 3:6). Making a donation is fundamental for empowerment. In the incarnational event, God made a donation of God's "only begotten Son that whosoever believeth in him should not perish, but have everlasting life" (John 3:16). Also in the kenotic experience described in Philippians 2, Jesus made a donation when he emptied himself of his divinity, robed himself in humanity, and became the chief servant.

Stewards, through their service, make a donation to kingdom building. The spirit and attitude that must fill us as servants of Jesus Christ is "such as I have give I thee." Some people concentrate so much on what they don't have that they never see the potential and possibilities of what they do have. Peter and John made a donation to this lame man who languished at the temple gate Beautiful begging for his bread. Imagine life from his vantage point at the bottom, always looking up to those who might see him with eyes of compassion and a heart of mercy enough to make a small donation. Certainly there were those who out of indifference never even saw this seemingly permanent piece of the gate. And undoubtedly there were others who joined him at the temple gate Beautiful to form an assembly of agony that caused the callous and cold-hearted to avoid this entrance entirely. Why go through this ghetto to get to God?

The church must first see the poor and oppressed as Peter and John saw this lame man begging for his bread. Seeing the poor that are with us always is the first step toward helping them. Our own positions of power and prestige can cause us to become blind to those at the bottom of the socio-economic ladder. Our own possessions and prosperity at the upper levels of humanity's house can render us oblivious to those trapped in the basement. When we see them, their problem becomes our problem. The "problem of the third world" is really the problem of the first world if we properly see that our world is a global community.

Our failure to see has allowed us to play the game of "out of sight, out of mind" with the 2.5 billion poor people of the world. I think we would be propelled into action as advocates of the poor if we were made to see ourselves where they are. Those who have eyes to see, let them first see. In a dramatic way, Robert Heilbroner describes in his book *The Great Ascent* what would happen to an American family if its standard of living were to be reduced to that of the underprivileged people of the world:

We begin by invading the house to strip it of its furniture. Everything goes: bed, chairs, tables, television set. We will leave the family with a few old blankets, a kitchen table, a wooden chair ... The box of matches may stay, a small bag of flour, some sugar and salt. A few moldly potatoes already in the garbage can be rescued, for they will provide much of tonight's meal.

The bathroom is dismantled, the running water shut off, the electric wires taken out. Next, we take away the house. The family can move to the toolshed. Communications must go next. No more newspapers, magazines, books ... Next, government services must go. No more postmen, no more firemen. There is a school but it is three miles away and consists of two rooms. They are not too overcrowded since only half the children in the neighborhood go to school.

The nearest clinic is ten miles away and is tended by a midwife. It can be reached by bicycle provided the family has a bicycle, which is unlikely.... Finally, money. We will allow our family a cash hoard of $5....[2]

After seeing this lame man, Peter and John then commanded the man to "look on us." Why? Perhaps because this man needed to have his sight lifted beyond just another coin or two. Perhaps he needed his hopes heightened beyond the basement level of life. He needed to see these servants of God with the afterglow of the Spirit on their faces and not consider them just some more passersby who threw a token coin in his basket out of duty rather than devotion. Will the church become so empowered by the Holy Spirit as to invite the "least of these" to look at it not as a museum for saints but rather as a hospital for sinners? Do the poor see the church as a community of hope and healing or just another country club closed to them and their problems? Too often the church is just another building blending in with others to make another city block of blight and banality. The church must tell the disenfranchised of society, "Look on us for a donation that will make a difference in your life."

The twenty-first-century church must also be willing to be a pioneer in its efforts to reach the poor, like the disciples of the first century were. Peter and John were bold in their thinking, courageous in their actions, and radical in their approach to giving this man not what he needed for his next meal but what he needed for a whole life. And surely the power of the Spirit must be employed by the church to go beyond customary collections and to help the poor break the bondage of bare subsistence.

The radical power of the Spirit will also enable the church to assume a prophetic presence in society in solidarity with the poor. The poor can't just be pushed into oblivion. They are an ever-present reality just as much as the rich, who are also present with us always. As long as there are rich people, they will by definition make others poor. But poverty is never that simple. As Douglas John Hall states, "Poverty is a complex amalgam of physical and spiritual pain, which robs the person and the community of dignity and meaning as much as it deprives the body of nourishment, shelter and beauty."[3] How can the first- and second-world's greed be justified in light of the third- and fourth-world's need? As faithful stewards, we in the church must condemn greed and exploitation, which create intractable pockets of poverty, and must work for an equitable distribution of the world's resources.

African Americans must especially be heard in this resounding symphony singing a new song of stewardship for the new world order. We especially are called to make a donation of righteousness and resources to the "least of these" that grows out of the rich soil of our unique spiritual and social struggles in America. Those who are downtrodden and forgotten, who never even had a chance to be caught by the so-called safety net because they were already below it, these are our brothers and sisters. They need this donation to be lifted up and liberated from sinful social structures and systemic oppression. This new song that we must sing will emphasize the theme that "the earth is the LORD's and the fulness thereof; the world, and they that dwell therein" (Psalm 24:1) so that all the families of the earth can share in the global treasures of God.

In making our donation, we must never forget that important spiritual law that "nothing can come into us unless it can get out of us."[4] Socrates observed this same principle when he stated that learning hasn't truly occurred until it is expressed in our behaviors and actions. In other words, the gospel demands an outlet before it can find an inlet. It's like the Sea of Galilee, which receives at its northern end the sweet, soothing waters of the Jordan River. The Sea of Galilee has not only an inlet but also an outlet to the south, whose waters create the fertile Jordan River Valley. In contrast, the Dead Sea is also fed by the Jordan River, but it has no outlet and therefore cannot support life within or without— and around it is nothing but desert. That's why it's called the Dead Sea.[5] This is the problem with so many Christians. They are always receiving but never giving. They are always wanting a blessing but are never willing to be a blessing. They have a cluttered outlet and therefore a closed inlet. Faith can't get into us unless it can get out of us. Hope can't get into us unless it can get out of us. Love can't get into us unless it can get out of us. The more we give, the more we have room to get.

They made a donation.

Second, *they added a stipulation to the donation.* They said, "In the name of Jesus Christ of Nazareth rise up and walk." Good stewardship demands that stipulations be added to our donations because everything we do we do by God's grace and for God's glory. Colossians 3:17 tells us that "whatsoever ye do in word or deed, do all in the name of the Lord Jesus, giving thanks to God and the Father by him." As good stewards, they added the stipulation for spiritual integrity and personal accountability. They wanted the lame man to know unequivocally that this was not by their power or by their might but by the power of Jesus Christ through them. The stipulation exemplified their spiritual integrity and magnified their Savior. Stipulating their source and themselves as his instruments avoided a potential explosion from the escaping gas of burning egos that has produced so much spiritual wreckage and so often sabotaged our success as stewards. Dr. Gardner C. Taylor has noted that when the civil rights movement was severed from its spiritual roots, it lost its spiritual integrity and social power.

Peter and John also made a stipulation for personal accountability. They wanted the lame man to help himself by using his own faith to rise up and walk. They realized that this man had come to accept his reclined position as his permanent posture and the temple gate as his permanent place and begging as his permanent profession in life. He had become accustomed to being carried through life, so he had to be challenged to probe his own potential and possibilities. Our stewardship is fundamentally a partnership, an accountability not only with God but also with each other.

If we are to truly help the poor, we must go beyond the Band-Aid approach of treating symptoms with anesthetizers and tranquilizers. Peter and John could have given the customary donation and proceeded into the temple. This would have left the lame man in his same condition, with only an instant of gratitude for another coin or two. Instead they made a donation with a stipulation of self-help. This radical reorientation of reality as he had known it resulted in a revolution in his life. While the Great Society social programs of the 1960s represented an admirable stewardship of national resources to ameliorate poverty, we now understand that more needed to be done in partnership with the poor. Economist E. F. Schumacher has said about empowerment of the poor:

Give a man a fish ... and you are helping him a litle bit for a short while; teach him the art of fishing and he can help himself all his life. On a higher level, supply him with fishing tackle; this will cost you a good deal of money, and the results remain doubtful; but even if fruitful, the man's continuing livelihood will still be dependent on you for replacements. But teach him how to make his own fishing tackle and you have helped him to become not only self-supporting but also self-reliant and independent.[6]

This partnership for liberation of the poor rests on the foundation of education. The first step in liberation is education. All involved must be educated to be set free from the prejudices, biases, and stereotypes that hold them in bondage. Education includes discipline and development. For empowerment the poor must be disciplined in the stewardship of their resources, no matter how meager they are. Too often this has been the missing element in our noble and genuine efforts to help the poor. Our donation will make a difference only with the proper stipulations.

The disciples' stipulation, rise up and walk, brings into further focus the matter of personal accountability. How many times have we squandered valuable resources by helping people get on their feet who never reached back to lend a helping hand to someone else. As Albert Schweitzer said, "They will not join the fellowship of those who bear the mark of pain." As stewards, we must avoid this American illusion of rugged individualism, this privatistic and pietistic approach to living the faith. This kind of sanctified selfishness makes us become obsessed with being successful at any cost rather than faithful at all cost. We get carried away by the firsts, but as Adam Clayton Powell said, what about the seconds and thirds? That's how you measure progress for a people. We suffer in the African American community because we have not added stipulations to our donations, and consequently we are prostituted by politicians and corporations who don't reciprocate with our fair share of the public goods and economic resources.

Finally, *we see a transformation.* Peter took this man by the right hand and lifted him up. Thank God for those who gave us a helping hand when we were barely existing down at the bottom of life! Somebody has said the only time we should look down on our brothers and sisters is when we look down to lift them up. The Scripture says that immediately his feet and ankle bones received strength. He felt his ankles, and they felt new. He looked at his feet, and they felt new too! He stood up for the first time in his life. He took one step and then two. He leaped for joy and then went into the temple to praise the God from whom all blessings flow. I can imagine he shouted, "I've been changed! I know I've been changed!" In the temple he must have said something like, "Lord, I thank you for remembering me, a lame man, lowly and among the least of them. But you lifted me. Thank you Lord for lifting me!"

As stewards, we proclaim to an unbelieving world that transformation by the power of God must begin at the temple. Transformation of modern man and woman and our world will not occur by the ideologies of capitalism, communism, or socialism but only through the power of Jesus Christ, who can change the sinful human heart into a heart of love toward God and our brothers and sisters. Even though this transformation is personal, it's not private. It begins with individuals but is always in the context of community. The church, in creating Martin Luther King, Jr.'s "beloved community," must transform society by liberating the oppressed so that justice will "run down as waters, and righteousness as a mighty stream" (Amos 5:24). Stewards are called to be salt in this day of decay and decadence. Stewards are sent forth as light in a dark and divided world. Stewards must show the love of God where there is hatred and hostility. Stewards will lead the way to life in a world bent on destruction and death. Stewards will model kingdom principles and priorities and usher in the new world order.

The great goal of stewardship is transformation—transformed people, transformed families, transformed communities, transformed nations, a transformed world. With such as we have, we must make our donations with the proper stipulations to see a transformation in the wilderness of this world that is crying for a voice that will proclaim the dawning of a new day, the coming of a new age, and the making of a new world. Stewards in service for Christ must be the voices crying in the wilderness in the tradition of the prophet who proclaimed, "Prepare ye the way of the Lord, make straight in the desert a highway for our God. Every valley shall be exalted, and every mountain and hill shall be made low: and the crooked shall be made straight, and the rough places plain: And the glory of the Lord shall be revealed, and all flesh shall see it" (Isaiah 40:3-5). Stewards must be ready for God's transformation. God "shall judge among the nations, and shall rebuke many people: and they shall beat their swords into plowshares, and their spears into pruning hooks: nation shall not lift up sword against nation, neither shall they learn war any more" (Isaiah 2:4). Stewards will rise up and walk in God's grace and for God's glory.

All scripture quotations in this sermon are from the King James Version of the Bible unless otherwise noted.

What's Your Life Worth?

Laura B. Sinclair

Someone in the crowd said to him, "Teacher, tell my brother to divide the family inheritance with me." But he said to him, "Friend, who set me to be a judge or arbitrator over you?" And he said to them, "Take care! Be on your guard against all kinds of greed; for one's life does not consist in the abundance of possessions." Then he told them a parable: "The land of a rich man produced abundantly. And he thought to himself, 'What should I do, for I have no place to store my crops?' Then he said, 'I will do this: I will pull down my barns and build larger ones, and there I will store all my grain and my goods. And I will say to my soul, 'Soul, you have ample goods laid up for many years; relax, eat, drink, and be merry.' But God said to him, 'You fool! This very night your life is being demanded of you. And the things you have prepared, whose will they be?' So it is with those who store up treasures for themselves but are not rich toward God." (Luke 12:13-21)

We all have watched at one time or another a little ant hill, with ants busy working as though there were no other world beyond their own. So it is with this man who spent his life, and spent it happily enough, getting and spending, gathering and consuming, pulling down and building up again—until that other life and that other world thundered in on him.

Laura B. Sinclair is associate executive minister for the Parish Resource Institute, American Baptist Churches of Metropolitan New York, and assistant pastor of Antioch Baptist Church, Corona, New York. She works with several young adult ministries and is a frequent speaker at churches throughout the country.

You know how it is. We go to school and get the best education. Then we spend our time getting the best job to earn the most money and highest prestige. We take time to look for our mate, that special person, that mister or missis right. We have children, buy a house in a good neighborhood in which to raise our children. If we stop and think about it, we realize that most people measure us—and we measure ourselves—by what we have and not who we are.

What is the lesson to be gained from this parable? Jesus wants us to know that it was not what this man had but what he lacked that was his undoing. He had plenty of money and goods. He was rich, as society would label him, but he was not rich in the sight of God. His thoughts went only to building himself another barn. Never once did he think of sharing his wealth. So while the world called him a successful man, God called him a fool.

This man was leading a disastrous, foolish life because of his hopes and expectations. He had reached the point that most of us look forward to. He had worked hard, and now he was about to retire. I'm sure he had been looking forward to this day for a long time. He had decided that when his new barns were built, he would eat, drink, and be merry. How natural it was for this man to feel this way! And how foolish was his thinking because of its false security!

This man thought that he had a long life ahead of him. He had locked the door against poverty. The *necessity* to work any longer had passed; the *anxiety* that comes with working had also passed. You know that anxiety, the one so prominent in today's society, the one that leaves you each week wondering if this is your week for the pink slip? Is this the week that I'm going to get sick? Is this the week that my car is going to die on me? Is this the week that I'm going to hear from my child's teacher about his or her behavior? Anxiety! It's known all too well to all of us. Well, all this had passed for this man. He was about to retire. He had made provisions for his retirement and was ready for all the benefits his hard labor had afforded him. He had prepared well. He was going to sit back and relax.

The one problem with all of this was that he did not stop to think that tomorrow might not come, that God would come and serve him a "pink slip" instead—a "pink slip" of no return. He had made no preparations for his salvation. He had forgotten about God. He forgot even to acknowledge what God had allowed him to do. He neglected to understand that he needed to prepare for his eternal life with God. The author of Luke-Acts is quite concerned that we understand the importance of preparing for our life with God as well as preparing for our earthly life. He was concerned that the Christian communities were in danger of assuming an attitude of covetousness. Through this parable he shows us Jesus teaching about the futility of storing up for the future when the future could be cut off at any time. Jesus shows us that serving riches is worthless when compared to serving God. That is why he said, "One's life does not consist in the abundance of possessions" (Luke 12:15).

Luke shows us further in Acts 2 and 4 that there is a mission theology that will help us through this dilemma. This mission theology is the necessity of alms giving and friendship. It shows us that the essence of the Way, the following of Jesus, is that Christians treat one another like friends, that giving possessions and caring for one another is extremely important in a life of faith. Luke makes it clear that the abundance of possessions can tempt us to become hoarders and make us unable to give alms. I believe that is what happened to the man in our story. His possessions caused him to neglect his responsibility to the poor and those in need.

Several years ago I met a man who had worked hard as a postal carrier. He worked for thirty years and gained a lot of material things. He was good at giving and working in the church in his early years of work at the post office. After working for about twenty years, he was able to pay off all his debts. He began to acquire material items. He collected Lladro porcelain, had three cars, three homes (two he rented out and one he lived in), and clothes galore. He was married and had five or six children. He had obtained everything he wanted, including a summer home, where he planned to spend his retirement years tending a garden and caring for some farm animals. The more he acquired, the less he paid attention to his tithes, both financial and spiritual. He stopped spending as much time in church because he said he had to take care of his possessions. He had to wash the cars. He had to dust his collection and be the caretaker for his homes. At age fifty-five, he reached his thirtieth year at the post office. He was ready to retire. His family gave him a retirement party one Saturday, and on Sunday he died. God said, "You fool! This very night your life is being demanded of you. And the things you have prepared, whose will they be?"

Are we required, therefore, never to have any possessions? Luke 14:33 looks as though one must give up all, but a clearer understanding of Jesus' teachings would be that we must be *ready* to renounce our possessions. This means that we must be willing to give up what we have, not that we actually have to give it all up. The willingness *must* be there, however, because on your walk with Jesus you might be required to give up your possessions. If you are able to give them up, you will then be willing to share your abundance. If you are not attached to your possessions, your possessions don't own you, and you will not neglect the poor. You can make your provisions for retirement and even enjoy what you have acquired, as long as you remember to share your abundance with those who are indigent, those who lack the necessities, those in need of alms. Be willing to share that which might be required to aid them.

Be able to do this with a genuine concern for the poor and a genuine love for Jesus, and you will find that you will not only be successful or rich in the eyes of society, but you will be rich toward God. You will have made proper preparations for the kingdom here and, most of all, for the kingdom to come.

70

You will be ready when death serves your "pink slip" because you won't be attached to this earthly life and you will have shared as God so desires.

Will you be ready when the death angel comes? Will you have made the proper preparations? Or will the Lord say to you, "You fool, this night your life is being demanded of you"?

All Scripture quotations in this sermon are from the New Revised Standard Version of the Bible unless otherwise noted.

AIDS and the Stewardship of Aid

G. Daniel Jones

"If my people, who are called by my name, will humble themselves and pray and seek my face and turn from their wicked ways, then will I hear from heaven and will forgive their sin and will heal their land." (2 Chronicles 7:14)

The word *AIDS* haunts us. AIDS, first diagnosed in 1981, has become a household word. Fear fills the atmosphere. Across the land and around the world, poor and rich, red, yellow, black and white, homosexuals, bisexuals, heterosexuals, asexuals, the sexually promiscuous, intravenous drug users and abusers, the users of shared needles and syringes, the unborn of the previously mentioned, health-care workers, dental patients, and, on occasion, recipients of blood transfusions, are all at risk. Victims of assault and rape are at risk. Whether attacked in prison, on the street, by burglary or kidnapping, the victims are at risk.

During the early 1990s, 1.5 million U.S. citizens were infected, with a steady increase worldwide. The most current study at the International AIDS Center based at the Harvard School of Public Health estimates that 2.6 million people around the world already have full-blown AIDS, and 13 million are

---

G. Daniel Jones is senior pastor of the Grace Baptist Church of Germantown, Philadelphia, Pennsylvania. He is a member of the general board of the American Baptist Churches in the U.S.A. and is second vice moderator of the Philadelphia Baptist Association. He taught in the department of Philosophy and Religion of Norfolk State University and was an adjunct professor in the Lilly Foundation's Ministry to the Black Church at the Virginia Union University School of Theology.

infected with HIV, the AIDS virus.[1] Dr. Jonathan Mann, former director of the World Health Organization and current director of the International AIDS Center, has predicted that by the year 2000, between 38 and 120 million people will be infected globally.[2]

As we approach the twenty-first century, the Harvard study reports that fifty-seven countries are considered high risk for spread of the virus, including Indonesia, Egypt, Pakistan, Bangladesh, and Nigeria, while thirty-nine other countries are identified as at substantial risk for a major HIV epidemic. By the year 2000 the largest proportion of HIV infections will be in Asia—42 percent. To date the infections in Africa have tripled to 7.5 million, spreading even further to the Caribbean and Central and South America. Our geographical borders do not make us immune, isolated, or insulated.

The U.S. Center for Disease Control has recorded that while African Americans make up 12 percent of the U.S. population, African Americans make up 28 percent of those living with AIDS.[3] The death rate continues to rise among people of color. The fastest growing population testing positive for HIV is the African American female. The April 1992 *Ebony* states:

> According to the Center for Disease Control of all people [in the U.S.] diagnosed, totaling 206,392, almost ⅓ are Black (60,037). It was projected that in the U.S., during the early 1990s, 270,000 persons will have had AIDS and 179,000 will have died. In New York and New Jersey, AIDS is the number one killer of Black women aged 15–44. More than half (52%) of all women with AIDS is Black, rising from 4.4 to 10.3 per 100,000 nationwide. The children with AIDS number 3,471 and of this total 53% is Black (1.844). The statistics concerning newborns with AIDS include a Black [populace] of 58%, and 60% of all pediatric cases. Almost 1 out of 4 men diagnosed with AIDS is Black (25%).[4]

What is AIDS? It is an acronym for Acquired Immune Deficiency Syndrome. AIDS is a virus that attacks the body's immune system and prevents it from fighting infections. AIDS is an infectious, contagious disease. The incubation period is anywhere from two to ten years. AIDS is fatal. Currently, to be infected with the AIDS virus is to be terminally ill. There is no known cure on the eve of the twenty-first century. It remains a worldwide public-health concern.[5]

AIDS Related Complex (ARC) is a condition caused by the AIDS virus in which the patient tests positive for AIDS but has no specific set of clinical symptoms.[6] Magic Johnson was in the ARC stage when he played basketball in the Olympics within the first six months following his announcement of his infection and resignation from the Los Angeles Lakers.[7]

In the midst of the AIDS epidemic is a clear call for loving, Christian stewardship. AIDS confronts us with the need for a stronger emphasis on stewardship of public health, health care, prevention, treatment, and work toward developing a cure. Wallace E. Fisher, in his book *A New Climate for Steward-*

ship, states that the congregation's responsible care of persons in its fellowship and its concern for those outside its fellowship are primary strands in biblical stewardship.[8] A congregation's effective care of persons inside its fellowship and concern for persons outside its fellowship are also measured by the biblical content of its formal preaching and teaching.[9] To care for another human being is to provide for his or her whole person, to attend to that person's full needs (physical and spiritual) by offering Christ's fellowship.[10] "To be a Christian steward is to follow where God leads by the abilities and strength he gives."[11] As Christ was faithful in his stewardship, so are we expected to be faithful. Faithfulness begins with the Great Commandment: loving the Lord our God with all of our heart, soul, mind, and strength; and loving our neighbors as ourselves.

The church is called to respond. The black church especially is called to awaken. What can the church do? The Christian is called to be concerned, to be involved, to be compassionate, to provide goods and services for persons and families living with AIDS, to push for research and national health care with more governmental and ecclesiastical involvement, which includes both the public and private sectors. The church at large is also called to demonstrate love and compassion for the infected, to plan and implement concerted action by placing pressure on the government, researchers, the medical field, the health care providers, and to discourage any form of oppression, discrimination, deprivation, dehumanization, or disenfranchisement.[12]

The Scripture lesson in 2 Chronicles 7:14 speaks to us. Stewardship is suggested in the first three directives, and God's promise of forgiveness and healing concludes this passage:

"If my people, who are called by my name, will humble themselves and pray and seek my face and turn from their wicked ways, then will I hear from heaven and will forgive their sin and will heal their land."

We Are in It Together.
(Identify with the Problem)

"If my people who are called by my name." During the early 1980s, AIDS was considered to be a disease that affected "them"—and not us. Who were "they"? In the U.S., the disease was first noticed among the middle-class, white, homosexual community. "Them" not us. The "they" spread to other "theys," including i.v. drug users and hemophiliacs. Now "they" are moving in closer and closer. The heterosexual population is affected more and more. Today the spread is including more of us, not "them." Each year since 1985 at least one of our parishioners has died of AIDS. Two contracted the virus from blood transfusions (a female senior citizen and a young adult male who had received transfusions all of his life); two were intravenous drug users (a male and a female); three, practicing homosexual males; another was a native of a high risk locale. It is no longer "them" but "us." Our spouses, parents, children, siblings, friends, uncles, aunts, nieces, nephews, cousins, neighbors, and coworkers are at risk.

As a pastor, I have observed three mothers who selflessly gave to their sons who tested HIV positive. They gave birth to them, nurtured them, watched them grow from infancy and mature into adulthood. These women of strength are models of maternal love at its best. Unfortunately, they had the painful experience of watching their sons deteriorate, decline physically, and fall into complete dependency. Following the deaths of their sons, one has withdrawn, closed this chapter of her life, and removed herself from any further involvement in the lives of others who are similarly suffering. The second mother is committed to championing the cause of AIDS education; attends seminars and workshops; and is a strong advocate for community, church, and government involvement. The third, mother of an only child, was shut in for over a year caring for her son. She is appreciative for the ministry of her church and is found serving, volunteering, worshiping, and assisting wherever possible. The church represented the presence of God in her life during her crisis, and she is spending the rest of her days giving thanks by being a blessing to others. It is not "they" but "we"—not "them" but "us."

When a son is infected, devoted fathers as well as endearing mothers are hit and stricken with indescribable pain, hurt, shame, and loss of esteem. Often dads who had much hope for their sons wonder where they have failed as parents. Unfortunately, due to ignorance, the infection carries a community stigma, coupled with fear.

Two fathers were observed in our congregation. One father was estranged from his only son, who lived a gay lifestyle in a distant metropolitan city. One year before the HIV-infected son died, he had returned to his parents. This was a period of healing and bonding. The son united with the fellowship of the church, was received and supported. It was a necessary time of reconciliation. Another father and son had a different experience of healing and bonding. Like the prodigal son, this particular son hit rock bottom in a distant land. He returned home penniless, jobless, hopeless, broken, and physically unhealthy. Upon returning, he was received with love, but never told his parents of his AIDS diagnosis. He visited his pastor, possibly with the intention to share his concern, but completed his conference without mentioning his illness. As time passed, his symptoms increased and his parents, who suspected the worst, forcibly had him examined. Their fear was confirmed. Dad was broken but dependable. Dad was hurt but was there. Dad was upset but was struggling with a situation beyond his control. He had always provided and cared for his family. The parents were mutually supportive of each other and of their son. The entire family rallied. When all else fails, love still stands. AIDS has hit home—"us" not "them." "Us" is an inclusive word. "Us" means everybody is susceptible. Everyone is at risk. *We are in it together.*

Angela Mitchell, in her article "AIDS, We Are Not Immune," in the November 1990 issue of *Emerge* magazine, eloquently writes:

> AIDS can no longer be dismissed by African Americans. Traveling the route from i.v. drug users and their sexual partners to unsuspecting members of our community, the deadly AIDS virus is finding its way into our bodies, our homes, and our lives.

AIDS in the black community is found more and more among the heterosexual population. Of those African Americans diagnosed with the AIDS virus, 50 percent is heterosexual. No one is exempt. The virus is threatening all who breathe and tread the globe. *We are in it together.*

Although the AIDS virus was first discovered in the United States among the gay community and intravenous drug users, it is a "cheap shot" to say this virus is the wrath of God toward this population. While such behaviors and lifestyles are questioned by many, the sins of the nation and world are so much broader. Israel was unfaithful to God; Solomon and his successors went from riches to spiritual rags. The U.S. and other strong nations have oppressed the poor and exploited the disadvantaged. If we have done it to the least of these, we have done it unto him, says Christ who is the Son of God. We show evidence of having turned away from a covenantal relationship with God. We have entered into war and killed innocent lives. We have worshiped other gods (including power, politics, economics, sex, popularity, the media, success, material possessions, chemical dependence, and many others). We wink at homelessness, smile at world hunger, and joke about immorality at all levels. We have polluted God's waterways, destroyed rain forests, polluted the air. We have corrupted young minds, molested children, contributed to the delinquency of minors. We have failed to give moral leadership. Globally, we are guilty of perpetuating societies that foster hedonism, racism, sexism, ageism, and classism. In many instances our business, ecclesiastical, educational, and political leaders have failed to remember who placed them in positions of responsibility and ultimately to whom they are accountable. Yet each of us, in some way, has failed to remember the holy covenant. Solomon failed, Israel failed, our current leaders have failed, and we as a people have failed. God expects more from his people.

A world in which the rich get richer and the poor get poorer at the expense and exploitation of the poor is distasteful to God. If only Solomon of the United Kingdom, Rehoboam of the Southern Kingdom, Jeroboam of the Northern Kingdom, and their successors had remembered the prayer of David in Psalm 51:

> Have mercy upon me, O God, according to thy lovingkindness: according unto the multitude of thy tender mercies blot out my transgressions. Wash

me thoroughly for mine iniquity, and cleanse me from my sin. . . . Create in me a clean heart, O God; and renew a right spirit within me. Cast me not away from thy presence; and take not thy holy spirit from me. Restore unto me the joy of thy salvation; and uphold me with thy free spirit (vv. 1-2, 10-12, KJV).

We have recklessly and ruthlessly engaged in war, destroying thousands of innocent lives. We have allowed international drug trafficking to go uninterrupted. Our borders need stronger protection and security. We have lost a strong sense of community, home, school, and church/synagogue. We have allowed the home and wholesome family life to deteriorate. We make a mockery of monogamous heterosexual marriages, while allowing ourselves to be entertained by acts of moral unfaithfulness and promiscuity. We are misfocused, misdirected, and misguided. There is widespread global misunderstanding concerning the power, presence, and commands of God. We have destroyed our own people, including farmers, steel and construction workers, mine and factory workers. *We are in it together.*

While Christ has been de-emphasized to satisfy those outside of the faith, including the atheists, our attention is being sought with an unwanted plague, a virus that falls on the just and the unjust. Some good people were placed in the Babylonian Exile. Some good people were enslaved in Egypt. Some good people were infected with leprosy. Some good people are infected with AIDS. Our attention must now be focused on the illness, on the virus. Our attention must turn to our only source of "aid"—establishing a right relationship to God. Globally, we are God's people; we are called by God's name. *We are in it together.*

We Can Work Together.
(In Communion While Dealing with the Problem)

"To humble ourselves and pray." This implies a divesting of self, a decreasing of self, in order to increase in Christ. It means to refuel with divine love by allowing oneself to be enveloped into the grace of God and by acknowledging dependence upon that divine gift of power in order to be a useful witness within the family of God. It means to decrease that Christ may increase, to be aware that we are related to fellow human beings by creation. This is a description of humility. From the Christian perspective, to allow Christ to move and work within us is operative humility.

To pray is to acknowledge a God who creates, directs, knows, hears, answers, and delivers. To acknowledge, adore, thank, petition, and intercede are summarized in communion with God, known as prayer. *"Humble ourselves and pray."* How does this apply to the subject of AIDS? It begins with our attitudes. Many of us either have been or tend to be judgmental. Some have inferred while others have stated that this infection might be an expression of the wrath of God for ungodly behavior. Such a punitive, judgmental, self-righteous response to a world crisis, a worldwide epidemic, is hardly appropriate. Instead, we must demonstrate a biblically based humility. Such humility is the way of Christ. Both unrighteousness and self-righteousness are detrimental to the soul and inhibit the growth of the kingdom of God on earth—and the kingdom of God within.

"Humble ourselves and pray." The truly humbled says, "I could be that person living with AIDS." The compassionate says, "One never knows, I could be any one of those persons living with AIDS." The prayerfully humbled knows that he or she is a part of all persons living with AIDS. It is not "they" but "we." It is not "them" but "us." John Donne wrote in his *Devotions* (XII, 1624):

> No man is an island, entire of itself; every man is a piece of the continent, a part of the main; . . . any man's death diminishes me, because I am involved in mankind; and therefore never send to know for whom the bell tolls; it tolls for thee.

"To humble ourselves and pray." The problem is beyond our own independent abilities to solve. Without God, without humility, without prayer, without a humble dependence on the power of the Almighty and a willingness to share and work with God's people, we are powerless. Prayer suggests the individual's need for divine intervention. Help from the Lord is our only hope. Help from above is our only cure. Prayer suggests and acknowledges to the Supreme Deity that we are limited. An outside force has challenged our abilities to cope or even survive. Prayer indicates that human hands reach for the divine hand. Humble human cries are heard by a divine ear. Humble human calls are answered by divine love and a heavenly voice. Jewish scholar Abraham Heschel states in *Man's Quest for God: Studies in Prayer and Symbolism,* "Prayer is our humble answer to the inconceivable surprise of living."

"To seek his face." No one has seen the face of God and lived, but Christ has been revealed to us. Through Jesus, the Word became flesh, dwelt among us, and we beheld the glory of God, full of grace and truth (John 1:14). That same Jesus reminds us that, if we have done it unto the least of these, we have done it unto him. The world has been brought closer not simply through the nuclear arms race; not through media, telecommunications, satellite, high-speed transportation; not by the United Nations' sessions and treaties; but through a disease that strikes irrespective of class, race, ethnic origin, nationality, economic status, sexual orientation, gender, or age. The disease is a threat to human survival. Either we live together as God's or we perish as fools.

"Seek ye the LORD while he may be found, call ye upon him while he is near," says Isaiah (55:6, KJV). The prescription for our survival may very well be in this text. Humble ourselves and pray—seek the face of the Lord and turn from our wicked ways.

"Turn from our wicked ways." The wicked way is the way of ungodliness. Wicked ways are behavior patterns and attitudes that are outside the will of God. Turn from displeasing God. Turn from sin. With respect to AIDS, wicked ways also include sins of omission, acting as though the problem does not exist. Sin is removing ourselves from any responsibility in alleviating pain, thus being a part of the problem rather than the solution. The proactively wicked ostracizes, shuns, criticizes, acts with scorn, and justifies judgmental responses. The un-Christlike spirit is wickedness. Un-Christlike behavior is wickedness. Expressing a lack of compassion is wickedness. We are to turn from our wickedness by not reducing others to mere objects, things. Turning from our wickedness is turning toward God, turning in favor of the spirit of Christ, and turning in the direction of Christian love. Love does not patronize. Love does not count the cost. Love does not expect thanks. Love does not condescend. Love is not snobbish. Love suffers long and is kind. Love loves for love's sake!

Wickedness is punishing the victim. Wickedness is blaming the victim. Wickedness is instilling guilt in others as well as self. Wickedness is cursing the darkness. Instead of cursing the darkness, in the process of turning from our wicked ways, may we light candles; discover electricity; replace blown-out bulbs by enlightening, educating, healing, and living in communion as children of the Most High God. *We can work together.*

We Are Invited to Live.
(Initiatives on God's Part in Solving the Problem)

"Then I will hear from heaven." We are invited to live in communion with God and in fellowship with Christ. Hearing from heaven is living. Living where God's Word is heard, obeyed, and followed—that's the kingdom, that's living within a new world, new creation, or new kingdom that is not of this world.

We all have a form of AIDS. We have spiritual AIDS. Our immune system has been destroyed by the infection of sin. Adam and Eve are the first victims of spiritual AIDS. In Adam all die. Sin is contagious. Sin is congenital. Sin is deadly. The fatality rate of spiritual AIDS—sin—is 100 percent. Because of the deadly infection of sin, other opportunistic spiritual illnesses surface, such as dishonesty, immorality, greed, selfishness, idolatry, envy, self-righteousness, inhuman interpersonal relationships, poor stewardship, and others.

Unlike those who test HIV positive, however, spiritual AIDS is curable. The body may go, but the soul can live. The body may be destined to die, but the soul can be saved now. There is a cure. However, you must believe that Jesus is Lord and Savior. Jesus saves! Jesus cures, touches, cleanses, heals, and reconciles. Spiritual AIDS has been curable since the crucifixion of Christ Jesus at Calvary in 30 A.D. One day, through Christ, there will also be a physical cure for those who test HIV positive. For a moment, or better still for eternity, let us prioritize. Let us allow Christ to enter our lives. Let us get right with God. Let us not insist on our own way. Let us humble ourselves and pray for ourselves and others. Let us seek the face of God by looking for God in the lives of others. Let us sow seeds of kindness and observe the Golden Rule. Let us turn from our wicked way of living outside of God's will and allow something positive to happen. Some breakthrough *will* occur. Some divine intervention *will* take place. Through humble, prayerful faith, returning to God, and turning from wickedness, mountains move; food drops from heaven; highways cross roaring seas without the aid of steel bridges or cement tunnels; rain pours for days following a drought; the leper is healed; the blind sees; the lame walks; and the dead resurrects.

"Forgive their sin." Forgiven sin is an opportunity to live. We are promised life. Being forgiven in order to forgive others is "realized redemption" and an expression of salvation itself.

"Heal their land." We are promised life. We are promised life of a high quality. A healed land is a land fit for habitation. A healed land is a land devoid of social illnesses, social diseases, and social problems. A healed land is a land free of misery, pain, and suffering. A healed land is a land inhabited with a healthy people reconciled to God. A healed land is a land of peace—peace of mind, a peaceful existence, and peace with God. A healed land is a Canaan experience. A healed land follows an enslavement, an exile, and an exodus experience. A healed land follows the humbling of ourselves, prayer pilgrimages, a turning from our wicked ways, a cleansing, purification, sanctification, reconciliation, and justification with responses in appreciation.

We are invited to live. We are invited to put a high value on universal health care. We are invited not only to love ourselves but to demonstrate love for others by assisting them in living, by improving the quality of their lives. *We are invited by Christ to live* faithfully as good stewards. Christ says to us, "I am the way, the truth, and the life" (John 14:6, KJV). *Invited to live!* He invites us by assuring us, "I am the resurrection and the life" (John 11:25). *Invited to live?* Jesus speaks, "I am come that they might have life, and that they might have it more abundantly" (John 10:10, KJV). *Invited to live!* A voice from heaven says, "I am the vine, ye are the branches" (John 15:5, KJV). *We are invited to live.* "In him was life, and that life was the light of men" (John 1:4). *We are invited to live* by Jesus, who clearly states, "Because I live, ye shall live also" (John 14:19, KJV). Because I live, do not become hopeless; do not slip into despair; do not live carelessly; do not live hopelessly; do not live promiscuously; do not put complete faith in condoms or the myth of safe sex; do not undermine sexual abstinence outside of marriage; do not mock health's safety precautions and the spiritual credibility of celibacy outside of marriage; do not put faith in the use of addictive drugs of any kind; do not put faith in temporary pleasure or immediate gratification at the expense of your own life or someone else's. The humbling of ourselves and praying, the seeking of the Lord's face and the turning from our wicked ways, the hearing from heaven, the forgiving of sins, and the healing of the land are processes in which we receive life, new life, abundant life.

In order to live, we must push for research, for an affordable antiviral vaccine, and a cure. *In order to live,* we must petition government to provide funds for research, treatment, and aid to persons living with AIDS. *In order to live,* we must demand that the work force, industry, government, municipalities, commonwealths, both public and private sectors, not discriminate against our brothers and sisters who are living with AIDS. *In order to live,* we must insist on exercising self-control against making poor social decisions and living unhealthy lifestyles. *In order to live,* we must emphasize the necessity of a change in behavior for the better. Social behavior as suggested in the New Testament is strongly recommended to be a key to survival. New creatures in Christ function in such a way that their priority is pleasing God with faith, attitudes, disposition, behavior, and service. "In him [Christ] was life, and that life was the light of men" (John 1:4).

In order to live, we must try it Christ's way—his ways are higher than our ways. His way is superior. His way is the way of holiness. His way is attainable. *In order to live* as people of God, we must provide model leadership for our parishioners, church communions, local communities, and subsequently for the nation and the entire world. *In order to live,* we must demonstrate our Christian love for those who are within the faith *and* for those without the faith. *In order to live,* our survival dependency must not be on self-medicated external stimuli, relying on addictive substances, resulting in addictive behavior, but we must have a concentration and a hope in the liberating Christ whose name is Jesus. We are capable of exercising self-control. We are created a little lower than the angels. We need to have minds that will stay on Jesus, and minds that are mindful of him. "For in him we live and move and have our being" (Acts 17:28).

In order to live, we must lift the fallen, help the weak and the poor, remembering that *we are in this together. We can work together. We are invited to live* and not to die. *We are invited to live* and not to cause death. We are invited to celebrate life, and not death. Even in a physically terminal state, *we are invited to live,* to value life, to ensure quality living, and to strive for new life in Christ as new creatures in Christ. *We are invited to live* with healthy bodies, minds, and souls, thus constituting a healthy existence.

Conclusion

Christianity is a faith that stresses resurrection, life, quality living, abundant living, including life with Christ in this world and life eternally with Christ. The apostle Paul says that living is Christ and dying is gain (Philippians 1:21). Remember, if the prerequisites stated in the text are honored, we can depend on God even while undergoing a threatening world epidemic known as AIDS.

Our land needs healing, and it shall be healed. Our bodies need healing, and they shall be touched. Our sinful souls need forgiveness, and we shall be forgiven.

Not every sick person or infected person has sinned to the point of causing the illness. Neither has every full-blown AIDS victim's parents sinned nor has every handicapped person's parents sinned as a rationale for the disability. In John 9:3, we read that *some* illnesses are permitted, as painful as they may be, so that the glory of the Lord may be revealed and the works of God might be made manifest.

When we come to the place of faithful stewardship where we humble ourselves, pray and seek his face, and turn from our wicked ways, then the glory of the Lord is being revealed and works of the Lord are being made manifest. When we submit to the will of God, though slain by circumstances and the wrecks of time, the glory of the Lord is revealed.

> Have Thine own way, Lord! Have Thine own Way!
> Wounded and weary, Help me, I pray!
> Power, all power, Surely is Thine!
> Touch me and heal me, Savior Divine!

After humbling ourselves and praying and seeking his face, then sins are forgiven and the land is healed in a miraculous way. Stewardship is honoring God by working with him, out of love for him, his people, his creation, and also out of appreciation for his unspeakable gift of salvation, presented in the person of Christ Jesus, his beloved Son. *Praise God!* The glory of the Lord is made manifest and is revealed when God's children cry out with the psalmist in Psalm 103:1-5 (KJV):

> Bless the Lord, O my soul: and all that is within me, bless his holy name.
> Bless the Lord, O my soul, and forget not all his benefits:
> Who forgiveth all thine iniquities; who healeth all thy diseases;
> Who redeemeth thy life from destruction;
>   [even AIDS, ARC, and HIV-positive testings]
> Who crowneth thee with lovingkindness and tender mercies;
>   [even when an infectious virus attacks my body]
> Who satisfieth thy mouth with good things . . .

While awaiting a miraculous cure, a miracle vaccine, or a miraculous healing, we are often tempted by Satan, as suggested by the frustrated, burned-out wife of Job, to "curse God and die." Yet, intercepted by a loving Savior, we regroup spiritually and gain satisfaction. After revival and regrouping, our youth is renewed like the eagle's, experiencing daily spiritual growth, receiving daily bread, acquiring daily coping power, building daily character, reflecting daily good rapport, striving to offer daily faithful stewardship, while at the same time calling upon the Lord, hearing his answer, responding to his Word, being encouraged by his promises and sustained by his love. In all areas of life we are called upon to be faithful stewards, depending upon, honoring, worshiping, and working with our God. *We are in it together; we can work together; we are invited to live.*

Thank You, God! Thank You, Jesus! Thank You, Holy Spirit! Thank You, Holy Trinity, Triune God, who by your sovereignty, forgives all of our iniquities and, in your own appointed time, heals all of our diseases. Amen.

All Scripture quotations in this sermon are from the New International Version of the Bible unless otherwise noted.

A Ministry That Prolongs Life

James C. Perkins

And he came and touched the bier: And they that bare him stood still. And he said, Young man, I say unto thee, Arise. And he that was dead sat up, and began to speak. And he delivered him to his mother. (Luke 7:14-15)

Throughout the long years of our pilgrimage on the earth, God has been seeking to impress upon us that it is his desire that we might have life, and have it more abundantly.

From that strange, mysterious moment in some distant, undatable day in the past, when God breathed the breath of life into the nostrils of a sculpted lump of clay, stamped his divine image upon it, and called it a living soul, God has blessed humanity with the gift of life and the necessary support systems to develop and sustain it.

A spiritual rumor has been about for centuries that the vaults and coffers of heaven are overflowing with treasures so exquisite that it lies beyond the capacity of the human mind to conceive or dream of them. Both Isaiah and Paul have reported to us that "eye hath not seen; nor ear heard, neither have entered into the heart of man, the things which God has prepared for them that love him" (1 Corinthians 2:9). But no matter how dazzling and glorious the unrevealed treasures of heaven may be, nothing in its inexhaustible storehouse can begin to compare with this precious gift of life.

We may not have everything we want. Our family may be falling apart. We may be frustrated in a dead-end job, our health may be failing, we may have

---

James C. Perkins is pastor of the Greater Christ Baptist Church in Detroit, Michigan. He is a member of the Detroit Pastors' Council and the Detroit NAACP and is founder and president of the Conference for Leaders of Black Church Youth Groups. He is past president of the Michigan Progressive Baptist Convention.

pain in our heart, tears in our eyes, and burdens to bear, but irrespective of these painful realities, it's still a blessing to be alive. When God touches us with his mercy and our eyes open to greet the light of a brand new day, we know that we are the recipients of the greatest and most cherished gift God has to give. The quality of our circumstances notwithstanding, life *is* a blessing. Life has its complex problems, yes, but it also has its infinite possibilities. Life has its stubborn obstacles, but it also has its awesome opportunities. Life has its grave injustices, but it also has its unfailing mercies. Life has its jolts, but it also has its joys.

God has designed life in such a way that it has no rival. Life is such a wonderful experience, life is such a glorious experience that its true essence cannot be measured by length of years, the balance in our bank book, or our socioeconomic status. Though it be lived for only a moment, life is the best gift God has to give.

Yet despite all that's wonderful and glorious about it, we seem to be passing through a perilous period when the idea of the sacredness and preciousness of life has fallen on hard times. A generation has risen up among us that appears to have declared war on life. Our streets have become combat zones, our homes have become prison cells, and each of us has become a potential target for violent elimination.

Life as God intended it was to be reverenced and respected above all else. But in these days, life is cheap. In these days, a life can be snuffed out for a little of nothing. In these days, a life can be taken just for the thrill of it. In these days, a life can be taken for a diamond ring, for a chain of gold, or for thirty pieces of silver.

A spirit of evil has seized the soul of this generation. Rather than being thrilled and challenged by the opportunities that life affords, young people are attracted and obsessed by the dark, dusty depths of death. Everything they prize already has the signature of death engraved on it. Their values are the values of death. They prefer profits to people, riches to righteousness, fame and fortune to faith and a future. And they'd rather try their luck than trust in the Lord.

How sad it is that our young people are dying so soon, in such large numbers, and in such violent ways! The infant mortality rate is higher among us than in some undeveloped countries. For us blacks, the life span has declined for the first time since mortality rates have been recorded. For us, if a black man lives to turn forty, it's almost a miracle. Death is all around us. Genocide, fratricide, homicide, or suicide. Whatever the cause, the result is the same. Death has declared war on us.

In our community, like nowhere else, death is big business. If you don't believe it, look around sometime and just notice how many funeral homes there are. There are funeral homes of all shapes and sizes. Some even look like great, sprawling, medieval castles. And they are all boldly competing for the enormous market of burying the dead. Death in the black community is not just a sad, tear-jerking event. Death for us is big business.

A funeral home can be a mansion with many rooms, while some churches have to remain a storefront. A funeral home can have a million-dollar budget, while some churches struggle to keep the lights on. A funeral home can have a fleet of hearses and limousines, while some churches can hardly afford a van. A funeral home can have a staff of ten or fifteen, while the church can hardly pay a pastor. A funeral director can be a millionaire, while some preachers have to work two jobs to make ends meet. In fact, some funeral directors have preachers on their staffs to dispense cheap hope and help wipe away costly tears. Some of us are willing to pay more for our funeral than we contribute to the church in the course of a lifetime. You can tell what condition the world is in by looking at the funeral home and looking at the church—the house of death and the house of life. When the funeral home is flourishing and the church is struggling, something is wrong.

Something has gone wrong in the world. Death was never intended to be the booming business that it is. Undertaking was meant to be done on the side by some benevolent soul who wanted to perform a community service. It was never meant to be lucrative enough to serve as a main source of livelihood. But death is having such a heyday that it looks like there's a better living in burying the dead than there is in preaching the gospel and trying to keep people alive.

One day all of us will have to walk the last mile of the way, see our last sunrise, enjoy our last party, have a last laugh, say a final farewell to family and friends, and go with that dreadful visitor whose presence is so profoundly felt among us. One day all of us will die, but we're not supposed to die until we've lived to a ripe old age.

When we study the miracles of Jesus, we will see that he performed the miracle of prolonging life. He raised three people from the dead. While each of these miracles has its own unique theological and hermenuetical message, the common message they all share is that God intends for us to live a long, full life. This is clear because all three of the persons whom Jesus resurrected were young people. He didn't resurrect any senior citizens (no offense intended) because they had lived out their allotted number of years. He raised up young people who had been tackled by death before they had had a chance to really live.

In the incident recorded in this text, Jesus demonstrates to his disciples both then and now that he expects us to develop a ministry that prolongs life.

He is entering the city of Nain. At the gate of the city, he comes upon a funeral procession. A young man, the only son of his widowed mother, is being carried to his final resting place. How often is this sad situation repeated in our community day after day? The father is dead and gone. The young men are not far behind. The wife is left to grieve alone and make it the best way she can. Meanwhile the church is sitting silently, looking on helplessly, and allowing death to have its way.

Well, the eulogy had been eloquently delivered. The choir had sung sweetly. The church clerk had read the cards, condolences, and resolutions. Now came the long march to the graveside for the service of committal. The grave is open and waiting. The grave attendant is awaiting the arrival of the company of mourners. The numb and grief-stricken mother is drowning in her tears. They're almost within burying distance when the hopeful word of our text reports that "the Lord saw her."

I'm so glad that Jesus sees us! Some of us never see anybody who needs our help. Some of us never see anything that needs to be done. Needy people and needy situations can be all around us, staring us in our face, and yet we don't see them. But the Lord saw her! She did not merely make an impression on the optic nerve of his omniscient eye; "The Lord *saw* her." He saw her weeping eyes. He saw her broken heart. He saw her dismay about tomorrow. "The Lord saw her."

And you ought to have the blessed assurance bubbling over in your bosom that the Lord sees you. He sees your hurts! He sees your hopes! He sees your anxieties! He sees your fears! He's got that kind of sight that looks beyond fault and sees need.

"When the Lord saw her," Luke says, "he had compassion on her." And we could do so much as a church and so much as individuals if we just had a little compassion. Our problem is that we just don't care.

At the gate of the city, life and death had an eyeball-to-eyeball confrontation. And life won out because the Lord of life saw and had compassion on a grieving soul. "And he came and touched the bier: And they that bare him stood still. And he said, Young man, I say unto thee, Arise. And he that was dead sat up, and began to speak. And he delivered him to his mother" (Luke 7:14-15).

Notice the actions and the consequence of the actions of our Lord. He saw. He had compassion. He came. He touched. He said. And he delivered.

Compassion motivated the Lord to move. He saw and had compassion, so he came. He didn't wait. And the church is just standing still when we ought to be moving. But we won't be on the move unless we see something to move for. We're not doing anything because we don't see anything.

In the action of our Lord, He is showing us that we ought to at least have enough compassion to get on the move and develop a *ministry that prolongs life.*

There are at least three elements in such a ministry that the church must do:

1. We must confront the condition.

"He touched the bier: and they that bare him stood still."

This bier was a wicker-like couch on which the dead were laid. It was against all religious and social custom to touch this bier, but Jesus touched it. He confronted the condition of death. If he had not been present with his disciples, they, like us, would simply have stepped aside and allowed the funeral procession in Nain that day to pass on its way. But Jesus refused to surrender this young life to death and the grave. He stepped in the way. He touched the bier, and the funeral procession came to a screeching halt.

Like Jesus, the church must confront the conditions around us that are carrying us to an early grave. We can't let death declare open season on us and then do nothing. We've got to bring our faith, spiritual gifts, and skills to bear on these death-dealing situations.

Jesus dared to confront death. He stepped up to death. He stepped in the way of death. He stretched out his omnipotent hand and stopped death. He touched the bier and the pallbearers stood still. Death kept pushing and trying to forge ahead. Death said to Jesus, "Move out of the way. I've got a hungry grave to feed." Jesus said, in effect, "Death, in order to do that, you've got to come by me." He touched the bier, and the procession stood still.

And if the church would touch the life of the dope addict, the dope pusher would be still. If the church would touch the lives of wayward fathers and wayward mothers, then wayward sons and daughters would be still. If the church would intervene and prolong life, then the undertaker would be still.

This was a bold, untraditional move on the part of Jesus. In the face of death, everybody felt helpless and hopeless and powerless. But Jesus confronted the condition—and stopped the funeral procession in its tracks. And if he did it then, he can do it now. Jesus has got the power to bring a halt to death. He can bring a halt to drug addiction. He can bring a halt to wasted days. Whatever it is, Jesus can bring a halt to it and give you a new lease on life. If we confront the condition, we can prolong life.

It doesn't matter what the problem is. It doesn't matter what the doctor says. It doesn't matter what society's prognosis is. Jesus can give you an extension of time. He's got eternity in his hands, and he can stretch time. He can stretch days into weeks. He can stretch weeks into months. He can stretch months into years. Jesus can prolong life.

2. We must give people an alternative.

"I say unto thee, Arise."

Not only must we confront the conditions that cause needless death; Jesus shows us here that we must also offer people a life-extending alternative.

Our people are caught up in a death-dealing lifestyle because the church has not worked hard enough to give them a life-preserving and life-extending alternative. Except for an hour or so on Sunday, the church is shut up for the rest of the week. We've got to build creative ministries based on the Word that teach people how to live, inspire them to live, and challenge them to see a higher vision of what their lives can become. They've got to know that there is no life apart from the Word of God because his Word gives life. If you want to live and know what living is all about, you've got to be brought under the authority of God's Word.

Jesus stepped up to the bier. He looked into the young man's face. There was a pallor in his cheeks. His eyes were closed in everlasting sleep. His arms were folded, never to swing freely again. I don't know how this boy died. I don't know if he was gunned down on the school ground because somebody wanted his Nike tennis shoes. I don't know if he OD'd in some cold, dark alley. I don't know if he died from AIDS. I don't know if he got sick of hypocritical folks and took himself out. Over here in Nain, he could have died from anything.

I don't know how this boy died. But I do know that Jesus stepped up. He leaned over, took out his divine key chain, and jangled the keys of Death and the Grave in the boy's ear. He said to him, "Young man, this is the Resurrection and the Life talking to you. I came that you might have life. I know Death's got a grip on you, but I can set you free. Young man, I say unto thee, I who am Existence Personified, I have no beginning and I have no ending. I say unto thee, I who turned on the primal lights and caused primordial darkness to gather up her skirt-tails and scamper into oblivion. I say unto thee. I who am the ground of all being. The omnipotent maker of all that is. The ultimate destiny of all that will ever be. I say unto thee! I who am all in all. I am swiftness in the foot. I am dexterity in the hand. I am strength in the arm. I am twitching in the eyelids. I am air in the lungs. I am every beat of the heart. I say unto thee! I am the mind's capacity to comprehend. I am the strong will's ability to implement. I am the soul's satisfied feeling. I am life. I am life in all of its abundance. I am the sum total of its component parts. I am life in the beginning. I am life in the middle. And when you get down there, I'll be at the end. I am Life. I say unto thee, arise! Get up! Don't stay stretched out in nonexistence. If you want to live, hear my word and arise."

The young man heard the word. The young man obeyed the word. And he sat up and began to speak. He spoke as a man who had staggered his way to life through the black fog of death. We don't know what he said. But we know he responded to the life-giving words of Jesus.

Only his Word can give life. Only his Word can give meaning to life. Only his Word has the answers to the existential questions of life. Where am I? How did I get here? Where am I going? His Word gives hope. His Word gives faith. Only his Word.

3. We must restore normal relationships.

"He delivered him to his mother."

Jesus is a great deliverer. After this great victory, Jesus delivered this young man to his mother. This is where he belonged. He was too young to be dead. At that point in his life, he belonged with his mother. Jesus delivers. Jesus reconciles. Jesus restores normal relationships. The church must do the same.

The breakup of our family life is abnormal. We need to build a ministry that prolongs life and restores normal family relationships. It's abnormal for young people to play cat and mouse with death as a lifestyle. Its abnormal for black men to go to jail so early and die so soon. It's abnormal for babies to have babies. It's abnormal for you to have a living body and a dead soul. Jesus can put broken marriages back together. He can put broken hearts back together. He can bring a dead soul back to life. Whatever the issue, Jesus delivers. Jesus restores normal relationships.

When Jesus resurrected this young man, Death got mad. Death leapt up off the boy. He kicked up some dust. He spit on the ground. He cussed a time or two. He pointed his long, bony finger in Jesus' face and said, "I'll get you for this one day."

Jesus responded, "Death, you meet me at Calvary, and we'll settle this living and dying business." Death went on out to the graveyard, and the waiting Grave and the waiting Grave Attendant were having a conversation. Grave asked Attendant, "Where is Death? He should have been here by now." Attendant looked up. He saw a trail of dust in the distance and said to Grave, "Here comes Death now." Grave asked, "Is anybody with him?" Attendant responded, "He's by himself." Grave said, "He must have bumped into Jesus. Ever since Jesus came to town, business has been slow!"

One day, Life and Death had a showdown at Calvary. Jesus hung on the cross and revived and restored a normal relationship between a forgiving God and a sinning humanity. Jesus got on the cross and invited Death to do his worst. The sun stopped shining. The clouds formed a black curtain around that hill of horror. For a while it looked like Death had conquered Life. Things looked dark all night Friday. Things looked dark all day Saturday. But bright and early Sunday morning, God the Father prolonged the life of God the Son. He conquered Death's sting and Grave's victory. He broke the back of Death. He died till Death died. He died that we might live. He died that we might have life and have it more abundantly. Abundant life, abundant faith, abundant grace, abundant peace, abundant joy.

> I serve a risen Savior, He's in the world today;
> I know that He is living, whatever men may say;

I see His hand of mercy, I hear His voice of cheer,
And just the time I need Him, He's always near.
He lives, He lives, Christ Jesus lives today! . . .
You ask me how I know He lives? He lives within my heart.*

All Scripture quotations in this sermon are from the King James Version of the Bible unless otherwise indicated.

Bread, Wine, and the Tithe

Milton E. Owens, Jr.

> You shall eat the tithe of your grain, your wine, and your oil, as well as the firstlings of your herd and flock, so that you may learn to fear the LORD your God always. (Deuteronomy 14:23)

More is said today about giving the tithe than eating the tithe. Perhaps "you shall eat the tithe" is a command that has been obscured by these words: "And those descendents of Levi who receive the priestly office have a commandment in the law to *collect* the tithe from the people" (Hebrews 7:5, italics mine). Tithing has come to be equated with the pastor begging, cajoling, even frightening church members into giving one tenth of their income to God.

Seldom is the tithe a call to break bread and drink wine in the presence of God. Seldom do we hear the tithe and the Lord's Supper being linked to each other. Many partakers of the Lord's Supper do not tithe, nor do they consider tithing to be an inherent part of the Lord's Supper. Tithing is considered an option and not a requirement. For many, a dollar for the general offering and a dollar for the mission offering is still considered a generous contribution.

Tithing began when Abram gave one tenth of all that he had taken from his defeated enemy. After partaking of bread and wine and being blessed by Melchizedek (king of Salem and priest of God), Abram gave his tithe to Melchizedek (Genesis 14:17-20). The biblical laws regarding the tithe required those giving the tithe to "eat the tithes of your grain, wine, and olive oil, and the first-born of your cattle and sheep. Do this so that you may learn to have reverence for the LORD your God always" (Deuteronomy 14:23, GNB).

Milton E. Owens, Jr., served as associated general secretary for the Office of the General Secretary, American Baptist Churches in the U.S.A. He routinely serves as an interim pastor for various churches in the Philadelphia area and a consultant to local organizations.

The tithe was established as an offering acknowledging God's ownership of the earth and all that is sustained by the earth—plants, animals, fish, and humankind. The eating of the tithe was a joyful occasion for remembering God as the source and owner of all the earth. The eating of the tithe was the recognition of an overwhelming need and dependence on God. The eating of the tithe in the place of worship was also an act of reverence toward God.

Today, in the tradition of Melchizedek, Jesus is the Priest-King over all, as proclaimed in the Letter to the Hebrews: "Jesus . . . has become a high priest forever, as the successor of Melchizedek. . . . Jesus, then, is the High Priest that meets our needs. He is holy; he has no fault or sin in him; he has been set apart from sinners and raised above the heavens" (Hebrews 7:15-26, GNB). As Abram took bread and wine from Melchizedek, so we partake of the Lord's Supper, the bread and wine that represent the body and blood of Jesus Christ, our High Priest, who sacrificed his life for all of humankind.

In that same tradition of Abram and Melchizedek, we should also present our tithe. Abram's tithe was given in celebration of his victory over his enemies. Our tithe ought to celebrate Jesus Christ's victory over sin and death:

> "Death has been swallowed up in victory."
> "Where, O death, is your victory?
> "Where, O death, is your sting?"

The sting of death is sin, and the power of sin is the law. But thanks be to God, who gives the victory through our Lord Jesus Christ" (1 Corinthians 15:54-56).

Our tithe ought to be offered in reverence for the Lord (Deuteronomy 14:23).

Yet in our computer-driven world, there are those who do not fully acknowledge God as the creator and owner of this world. Perhaps they have been persuaded by electronics and the "silver screen" that ingenious men and women are in charge of our world. Was it not men and women who created *The Ten Commandments* (the movie) and parted the waters? Are not men and women able to make things appear and disappear on the TV? Accordingly, some have come to believe that human beings are the source and owner of all.

What about churchgoers? Perhaps some steadfast churchgoers do not acknowledge God's ownership of all the world because they are not overwhelmed by a need and dependence on God. Maybe the steadfast churchgoers' unwillingness to acknowledge dependence on God is also their reason for not tithing. The tithe is an act of reverence for God as the source and sustainer of life. According to Deuteronomy 14:23, the tithe is to be consumed "so that you may learn to have reverence for the Lord your God always." So, why tithe when not overwhelmed by a need for God?

Sometimes the motive for not tithing is the erroneous assumption that the preacher gets all of the money for working only from 11 A.M. until 1 P.M. on Sundays, when the Bible says our tithe is the means of supporting those without property (Deuteronomy 14:27-29). Much has been said about the preachers who have abused their calls. Yet very little is made known about the majority of preachers who, though renumerated with little money, give much in being true to their call to preach and serve God's people.

In biblical times, the tithe was brought to the appointed place of worship and eaten in the presence of God by the tither and his family (Deuteronomy 14:23,26).

> Set aside a tithe—a tenth of all that your fields produce each year. Then go to the one place where the LORD your God has chosen to be worshiped; and there in his presence eat the tithes of your grain, wine, and olive oil, and the first-born of your cattle and sheep. Do this so that you may learn to have reverence for the LORD your God always. If the place of worship is too far from your home for you to carry there the tithe of the produce that the LORD has blessed you with, then do this: Sell your produce and take the money with you to the one place of worship. Spend it on whatever you want—beef, lamb, wine, beer—and there, in the presence of the LORD your God, you and your families are to eat and enjoy yourselves (Deuteronomy 14:22-26, GNB).

Many modern-day worshipers have come to accept the sale of tickets for church suppers, rallies, raffles, fashion shows, and other established fund-raising efforts as acceptable practices—although tickets, raffles, and rallies are not what Bible believers could term biblical. These fund-raising endeavors have resulted because worshipers have been unable or unwilling to tithe. Some churches would experience a significant growth in their treasuries if their one-dollar-a-week contributors would place seven dollars in the offering plate each Sunday—one dollar a day for the many blessings bestowed each day.

Although their relationship to the tithe has been obscured, church dinners are analogous to the command to eat the tithe. There worshipers continue to eat what is given in the tithe offering, but no longer with the solemn reverence to God as the source of all that exists. Reverence needs to return in the consumption of the parishioner's tithe. Sadly, instead, the church's budget is often a battleground, and there is little joy or celebration of God.

The tithe (offering) should be consumed by those who bring it. The church family should enjoy consuming its tithed financial resources to (1) sustain meaningful opportunities for education and fellowship; (2) sustain ongoing ministries for enabling each other to live successfully in an often cruel environment; (3) maintain a warm, comfortable, inviting house of worship; and (4) provide spiritual nourishment through worship, prayer, and Bible study.

Every third year, however, the people of God were required to share their tithe with "foreigners, orphans, and widows who live in your towns" (Deuteronomy 14:29, GNB). During the third-year tithe, all people in need were expected to come and eat all that they wanted, and God would bless the tithers. Perhaps Jesus claimed that the poor would always be among us because he knew the tithers would be few (Deuteronomy 15:11; Matthew 26:11).

In keeping with the command to tithe, the church must give of its financial resources for helping people in need who are residing in our community. What an impact the church could make on poverty, homelessness, medical care, hunger, and lostness if it were to institute the third-year tithe for any and all who were in need!

We are compelled to return to God our tithe, for we acknowledge, acclaim, and glorify God with profound reverence for sending Jesus to suffer and die for us. As made known in the book of Deuteronomy, "You shall eat there in the presence of the LORD your God, you and your household rejoicing together" (14:26). It is Jesus Christ's victory over death that we celebrate today. Let us joyfully bring our tithe to God in reverence and gratitude, and then partake of his bread and wine, our Lord Jesus Christ, in the presence of God and the household of faith.

All Scripture quotations in this sermon are from the New Revised Standard Version of the Bible unless otherwise noted.

To Practice

We Must Account for Our Stewardship

Johnny L. White, Sr.

Now He was also saying to the disciples, "There was a certain rich man who had a steward, and this steward was reported to him as squandering his possessions. And he called him and said to him, 'What is this I hear about you? Give an account of your stewardship, for you can no longer be steward.'" (Luke 16:1-2, NASB)

On April 12, 1992, at about 5:30 A.M., I had a dream or a vision about stewardship. To say the least, I was somewhat taken aback, for I had been laboring with the knowledge and awareness that I had accepted an assignment to do something (from a pastor's perspective) with the New Testament Greek on Christian stewardship. Upon brief reflection I decided to write a letter to "someone"—a close friend or acquaintance—concerning stewardship. May I presume you (the reader) to be my close friend or acquaintance?

Dear Friend,

I am writing to you on the subject of stewardship. One would naturally expect a person writing on such a subject to have some valued information to

---

Johnny L. White, Sr., is pastor of First Calvary Baptist Church of Norfolk, Virginia. He has served two terms as moderator of the American Baptist Churches of Virginia and has been on the personnel committee of the Executive Board of the American Baptist Churches of the South. He currently serves on the board of the Shaw University Divinity School, Raleigh, North Carolina, and has been a recognized advocate for public education.

share with others. More specifically, one would expect a pastor writing on stewardship to have "a stewardshiping church," which I have to conclude our church may not be. This awareness quite naturally backed me up and off the trail just a little bit. I know of some churches where, it is reported, "stewardship commitment" abounds. Maybe some of the spiritual tacticians giving pastoral oversight to these temporal structures should be sharing "how to do it" or "how not to do it" things with us.

I, along with so many of you, have sat at the feet of professors who sought to teach stewardship "from the book." The selected textbook contained "how stewardship should be done" things. Many of my early professors served churches close by the learning institution, so observing their ideas at work was easy to do. The late Dr. L. E. M. Freeman, a beloved professor of mine, used to tell us that it took many years for an idea emanating from the seminary or divinity school to get to the local church pew. I have found this statement to have a high degree of accuracy. I say this because most of the churches served by my professors did stewardship things the way many of our churches do them now—they do the best they can under the pressure of circumstances—that is, they still "rob Peter to keep Paul in business." Somehow or other there is rarely time to teach congregants how to do stewardship when the bills are due, the church building is caving in, and dysfunctional things keep popping up. So many of us, by necessity, have attained a high degree of proficiency in maintenance ministry, in "getting along somehow," rather than in a productive practice of ministry.

Across the years many clarion calls have been made to our members for things needed to operate the church. The responses have produced dinners (chicken, chitterlings, hog jowls); cakes, pies, pudding; patrons listings, bingo games, raffle tickets, contributions; and many other emergency stewardship devices or gimmicks. I make great haste to say that "emergency stewardship" as practiced in many of our local churches is not New Testament stewardship. One uses what one has, and one does what one has to do. Having accomplished the immediate goal, the evaluation of such is "It is finished. We did what we had to do; on to the next assignment."

But enough generalizing. What specifically is biblical stewardship? What specifically is New Testament stewardship? What is Christian stewardship? What is responsible stewardship? What is "common sense" stewardship?

There is no stewardship without the steward who is willing for the Lord to use her or his ship. *Steward* is a word used to translate a number of terms and expressions in the Bible. Common to all of these terms is the idea of overseeing the possessions, business affairs, property, servants, training of children, and so forth of an owner or master. A steward is one who is placed "over the house," or over business affairs (see Matthew 20:8; Luke 16:1-18). A workable definition of a steward is one who

manages the household or estate of God,
arranges a household,
manages, directs, and administers.

Stewardship carries with it the idea of

giving up or giving back,
restoring,
returning,
rendering what is due,
paying,
giving an account of.

Stewardship also includes the idea of handing over or giving up what is one's own. It means, in addition, to

give in or give way,
give a share of,
give before or first,
show favor or kindness,
give freely, bestow graciously,
give more,
give oneself to,
turn one's mind to, attend to,
fulfill one's household duties,
keep one's self in proper order,
utilize the best in management technology and techniques.

I have an unscientific idea, or feeling, that even in churches that are doing stewardship work, one act is categorized as stewardship—tithing. (A loose working definition of tithing is "giving a tenth of one's yearly income to the church [local or otherwise] to enable it more efficiently and effectively to carry out its mission.") This is no small accomplishment. It may suggest that in such churches where this is the situation, there is no great fear of not having enough money to do monetary things.

However, monetary things do not exhaust the meaning and mission of the Lord's churches. Tithing, though scriptural, though efficacious, is not all of our "household duties"—it does not fully exhaust the meaning of New Testament stewardship. There are other rooms in the house that we oversee. (More often than not, there are other persons in the house—mothers, fathers, sisters, brothers, children, the aged, the disinherited, the dropouts, the drop-out-ins, the pushed aside, and so on.) At least one room in the house is for time. Another room is for talents. Another room is for influence. Another room is for substance. Another room is for personality. Another room is for commitment. Another room is for mental construct (the house-arranging element). Surely, this word imagery should give a different look, and, hopefully, a different emphasis to our future efforts at stewardship.

Many Greek words describe the steward and stewardship:

oikonomos (the manager of a household or estate)

oikourgos (to watch or keep the house)

epitropos (the one who manages the house, a steward or foreman)

oikonomia (management of a household)

oikonomeo (to hold the office of an *oikonomos,* be a manager or steward; to regulate, administer, plan)

apodidomi (to give, hand over, deliver something to someone; to give up, surrender)

metadidomi (to give a part of, impart, share something with someone)

paradidomi (to hand over, deliver, entrust, give back, restore)

prodidomi (to give in advance)

charizomai (to give freely or graciously as a favor of God)

prostithemi (to add to something already present)

scholazo (to have time or leisure, busy oneself with, devote oneself to, give one's time to)

From the very beginning—clear to the end—the steward is a *doulos* person—a bond servant, a person serving under bondage to another. This *doulos* person owns nothing. This *doulos* person lives to please his or her owner. This *doulos* person has a lifetime challenge or task of "house arranging" or "house management"—managing God's house, overseeing the Lord's work—with the firm assurance that the Owner of the house will come back some day to assess both the housekeeper and the house.

First Corinthians 4:2 says, "Moreover it is required of stewards that they be found trustworthy" (RSV). Every steward must live with an awareness of tense and termination. This requires a close look at Luke 16:2, "And he called him and said to him, 'What is this I hear about you? Give an account of your steward-ship, for you can no longer be steward' " (NASB). One may presume, assume, or speculate that this person was once classified as a steward, only now to find that his or her employment is being terminated due to "*oikonomeo* malprac-tice." Consider having given a lifetime of service in house managing only to have the Owner come and declare to us that we have been derelict in the stewardship of the household and that there is no longer any need for our services—and there is neither time nor resources to make amends. My prayer is that this does not happen to any of us.

Even though teaching stewardship can be difficult, teach it we must. Even though doing meaningful stewardship is challenging, do it we must. It is not mandatory that we be successful; but we must be faithful. It is not written that we must succeed; but we must try to be faithful (and be faithful in our trying).

In this way we make ready for the coming of the House Owner. We make certain that we do not have to hear the House Owner say, "You can no longer be steward." Our workbook, the Bible, says in part, "Well done, good and faithful slave" (Matthew 25:23, NASB). This is stewardship well done. This is a faithful steward's "well done!"

Sincerely,

Your coworker in the Lord

A Pastor's Tithing Testimony

J. Alfred Smith, Sr.

"Will a man rob God? Surely not! And yet you have robbed me.
" 'What do you mean? When did we ever rob you?'
"You have robbed me of the tithes and offerings due to me. And
so the awesome curse of God is cursing you, for your whole nation
has been robbing me. Bring all the tithes into the storehouse so that
there will be food enough in my Temple; if you do, I will open up
the windows of heaven for you and pour out a blessing so great you
won't have room enough to take it in!" (Malachi 3:8-10, LB)

If a Jew gave one tenth under the Law, it is a disgrace for a Christian to give less under grace. Giving is a necessary part of Christian living. Percentage giving enables you and me to move up the giving ladder year after year, until we have at least become as the good Jew who gave the tithe.

Too many of us are like old Deacon Horner, who sat in the corner as the contribution box passed by. Sweetly content, he dropped in a cent and said, "What a good churchman am I." We who are American Christians are disgraced because God has given us so much, and we in return have given God so little.

Americans make up only 6 percent of the world's population. We possess 20 percent of its gold, 40 percent of its silver, 50 percent of its zinc, 60 percent of its copper, 66 percent of its oil, 40 percent of its railroads, and 85 percent of its automobiles. Yet, we disgrace our Christian boasting when we give less than the 10 percent that God commands and demands. This message is

---

J. Alfred Smith, Sr., is senior pastor of Allen Temple Baptist Church in Oakland, California. He is professor of Christian ministry at the American Baptist Seminary of the West and the Graduate Theological Union of Berkeley, California. He is past president of the Progressive National Baptist Convention, U.S.A., Inc., and has served as a member of the executive board of the National Council of Churches.

entitled "A Pastor's Tithing Testimony." Let me tell you why I plan to continue to obey Malachi 3:8-10 by tithing.

I tithe not because I have a surplus of money, not because I am out of debt, not because I fear that I will go to hell if I don't tithe, and not primarily because of a sense of duty—even though I feel I have a responsibility of love that requires that I give a tithe as a minimum. I tithe to God through Allen Temple in order to acknowledge divine ownership of all things I am and have. I believe with the psalmist that, "The earth is the LORD's, and the fulness thereof; the world, and they that dwell therein" (Psalm 24:1, KJV).

The Lord is our creation sustainer. As owner, God has a right to an increase from that which belongs to him. God has clearly stated what his minimum share should be: "And all the tithe of the land, whether of the seed of the land, or of the fruit of the tree, is the LORD's: it is holy unto the LORD" (Leviticus 27:30, KJV).

The Law asks for only 10 percent. The hotel and restaurant industry asks for a 15 percent gratuity. The prophet Malachi is even clearer in the words of our text, stating the amount that belongs to God. We must beware lest we labor under the impression that if we give the tithe we have met our financial obligation to God. Malachi 3:8 reads:

"Will a man rob God? Surely not! And yet you have robbed me.
" 'What do you mean? When did we ever rob you?'
"You have robbed me of the tithes and offerings due to me" (LB).

The Bible says tithes come first, then come offerings. Offerings are like icing on the cake. Some of us give the icing without the cake. And some of us give the cake without the icing.

I pay the tithe to God through the church because I believe that the tithe is God's method for financing the advancement of God's kingdom. Our Lord gave his church a commission with worldwide significance (see Matthew 28:18-20). In writing to the church at Corinth, Paul specifically referred to the fact that their offerings should be proportionate (see 1 Corinthians 16:2). No verse of Scripture even suggests that God's people should give less than 10 percent of their increase for the Lord's work.

I pay a tithe to God through the church because I want to be honest. I want to be honest in all of my business relationships. Most of all, I want to be honest with God. If the tithe belongs to God, I want God to have every cent of it. I do not believe that I can prosper by withholding from God that which belongs to him.

I pay the tithe to God through the church because it helps me be more Christlike. A Christian is one who is Christlike. Christ gave himself unselfishly for us. To buy us out of the slave markets of sin, Jesus left the riches of heaven and took upon himself the poverty of earth. So that you and I could become heirs to the riches of eternal life, Jesus came from the hails of heaven to the nails of the cross, from heaven's commendations to earth's condemnation, from heaven's honors to Calvary's horrors. What a price for Jesus to pay! He didn't have to do it, but thank God he did!

The law of heaven is love because God is love. My giving to God is an expression of my love for God, who so loved me that he gave his Son to die for me. The law of earth is selfishness. All of us have an inward inclination to selfishness. We are taught to get all that we can and to can all that we get. It is easy to believe that a person's life consists of the things that he or she possesses. The world encourages us to measure success in terms of the things that we acquire. God measures us in terms of what we give and the manner in which we give.

I pay the tithe through the church because I desire the blessings God has promised the tither. Part of the blessing of God to the tither comes in a satisfied conscience. I feel good knowing that I have obeyed my heavenly Father. A part of the blessing of God to the tither is the knowledge that through giving he or she has made evangelism and missions possible. I make the best possible investment when I tithe.

To conclude, I pay a tithe and bring an offering to the church not to try to pay God for blessings, but to say thank you to the Lord by giving generously to Christ. I say thank you, Lord, for your countless blessings. Thank you, Lord, for sweet Communion, for pardon, for your presence, for your power. Thank you, Lord, for providing for all of my needs. Thank you, Lord, for allowing me to serve you as a Christian steward. Most of all, thank you, Lord, for Jesus Christ, my Redeemer.

O God, we pray for security and, most of all, for courage to do your will. Help us to cherish as friends not those who make us uncomfortable but those who join us in the fight for truth and justice. Teach us to honor thee, not only with our voices but also with our lives and our pocketbooks. Send us doing, acting, and giving church officers and followers. In Jesus' name I pray. Amen.

Assessing Historical Financial Patterns of the African American Church*

Clifford A. Jones, Sr.

Historian Carter G. Woodson has documented at least five identifiable historical periods of the African Christian church in America. Each period focuses on specific goals in the development of the African Christian church in America. It is this writer's opinion that the term *church* is more historically descriptive than *black church*. The ethnocentric ethos of African culture and religion predate the term and phenomenon of what is called the black religious experience in America. The place of our birth is America, but our ethnicity is African, and one's ethnicity takes precedence over one's place of birth.

There are many Christian religious experiences in America: Presbyterian, Baptist, Methodist, Episcopalian, and others. Since I am a Missionary Baptist, much that will be said is from that religious tradition. However, the patterns of stewardship are similar throughout the historical development of the Christian experience in America.

This discussion will focus on three areas. First, because of the major role of the reverend in the Christian church, it is only logical to discuss this role relative to stewardship. In her book *Linden Hills*, Gloria Naylor provides a literary illustration of one attitude toward tithing:

"I hear Hollis's church is so slick they don't depend on no collection plates. They have this con game called 'tithing.' Roxanne thought about converting

---

*Adapted from "Stewardship from a Black Perspective" © 1988 by the Ecumenical Center for Stewardship Studies, 1100 W. 42nd St., Suite 225, Indianapolis, IN 46208. Used by permission.

once when she was into her nationalist fever. Said it was more black to be Baptist. But when she found out that all the members of Sinai were expected to give a tenth of their incomes to the church—before taxes—she decided to stay an Episcopalian and just grow an Afro."[1]

This quote reflects an attitude toward the church and tithing—and toward the reverend.

Second, the historical background and trends in giving will be discussed. What social, economic, and religious setting produced negativism toward the biblical concept of wholistic stewardship? This question will be addressed and another aspect essential to understanding stewardship from the Christian perspective will be considered: historical giving trends. For whom and what was the money raised? How was it raised? Why did members contribute to the ministry of the church, the building program, and support of the reverend, and give to the needy through the mission offering?

Finally, the summary will share observations about stewardship from the Christian perspective and seek to give some direction for developing a stewardship format. Often our failure in developing a stewardship format comes from not knowing the historical giving patterns of the local church and not being patient in developing an alternative.

The Reverend

Carter G. Woodson, in his book *The History of the Negro Church,* said,

The ministry too is more attractive among Negroes than among whites. The white minister has only one important function to perform in his group, that of spiritual leadership. To the Negro community the preacher is this and besides the walking encyclopedia, the counselor of the unwise, the friend of the unfortunate, the social welfare organizer and the interpreter of the signs of the times. No man is properly introduced to the Negro community unless he comes through the minister, and no movement can expect success there unless it has his cooperation and endorsement.[2]

This describes a perception of the reverend as more than a person like other persons. The reverend (historically the reverend was male) was "God's man"—God-called, God-ordained, and God's messenger among the people. Consequently, the success or failure of programs in the church and community depended on "a word from the pastor/reverend." The reverend was respected, yet often the punch line of ignominious jokes; loved, yet the object of disdain and envy; overworked and grossly underpaid. Meet Reverend Smith:

It was during the Depression. He had a church in a little country town called Stockard, Arkansas. They'd lost all their savings when the bank failed. He took another church in another little country town and traveled back and forth between the two trying to earn enough to make ends meet. The people didn't have any money either, but in the summer they paid him in tomatoes and turnip greens and chickens. In the winter, all the vegetables they canned that fall were about used up and he didn't know what they were going to do. . . .

Reverend Smith looked for odd jobs in Stockard and the surrounding towns. He'd done just about everything at one time or another—carpentered, farmed, taught school, barbered, been an undertaker's assistant, painted houses—but with white folks going hungry, who was going to hire a Negro?[3]

Contrary to many perceptions, the reverend did not receive "all the money." This misperception of the reverend is often used as a reason not to be intentional stewards. Reverend Smith is not atypical; his life has been lived a thousand times, and historically there was very little money. However, this misperception did not greatly hinder the reverend's influence in the church and community. This influence has been documented as three distinct developmental periods in the Christian church. These periods are as follows:

1. *The reverend of slavery and early freedom days.* There were few church buildings, and his leadership, along political, social, and religious lines, was to a nonliterate congregation.
2. *The reverend as organizer and builder.* This was a result of large migrations from rural to urban areas and from the South to the North.
3. *The reverend as fund-raiser and business manager.* With the acquisition of property, money was needed to pay the mortgage and for general maintenance costs.

During a meeting of the Valley Baptist Association in the late nineteenth century, Elder W. D. Woods, pastor of the Washington Street Baptist Church of Bedford City, Virginia, preached a sermon that aptly described the calling of the reverend as steward. The sermon, entitled "The Faithful Steward" (see pages 12-19), was based on 1 Corinthians 4:1-2 and included the following:

Dear fellow ministers, we have in our text a most helpful lesson. If we follow and practice it, we shall meet with greater success in our work for the Master. We have been called and appointed by the Lord Jesus Christ to fill a most important office, to perform a most delicate and onerous piece of work, that is, to stand between heaven and hell and call people to repent of their sins and return to God with faith in Christ and be saved from the destruction of their own vices and sins.

Historical Trends

Carter G. Woodson has identified five historical periods marking the embrace of the church by black Americans:

1. *The period of missionary endeavor,* in which white and black labored together
2. *The rise of independent churches,* 1773–1821
3. *The era of development,* 1821–1865
4. *The age of expansion,* 1866–1900
5. *The twentieth century,* when the black church became an effective instrument in black life[4]

These five stages reflect the pilgrimage of a people who were scarred, battered, and psychologically chained, yet full of hope, courage, faith, determination, and belief in a God known through the acts of "masa" Jesus.

These ebony children of God were nonliterate not because of aptitude and ability but because of their circumstances—slavery. Through trials and tribulations, they were coming up as domestics, sharecroppers, carpenters, blacksmiths, farmers, and mill workers. They formed congregations in rural, urban, and metropolitan areas across the United States. There was not a lot of money in these congregations because of the limited availability of jobs, the economic status of the nation, and attitudes of racism and prejudice. Yet, these congregations bargained to purchase buildings, construct new sanctuaries, and build fellowship halls and kitchens. These churches for the most part were deeply in debt. However, rural churches often "paid as they went" in order to avoid debt. The scenario for many early African American churches went something like this: a building was purchased, resulting in indebtedness, which led to fund-raising. The funds were usually handled by a deacon, and bills were paid as money was available. There was no budget, no savings account; these churches existed financially from Sunday to Sunday and hoped it didn't rain. The desire and will to be debt free was the driving force for giving to the church. The goal was ownership of the church, the first institution owned and operated by African Americans. The sons and daughters who started with strong backs and hands could then say, "Our church is paid for."

Money-raising, especially for debt retirement, controlled a large portion of the energy, time, and ingenuity of many congregations. This caused a considerable amount of concern, sardonic humor, and criticism from within the congregation and from the community. Demands increased as congregations purchased buildings, expanded services, encountered maintenance costs, and met financial obligations for the pastor. An elderly woman, reflecting on this new urgency and the constant appeals for money, said, "All the spirit done gone out of the church; money drove it out." Multiple collections were quite common, as were penny or sick offerings for pews (a special one-time effort). However, many members accepted this as a necessary pattern. Giving for some was a matter of competitive prestige and pride, and the amount given was often equated with faithfulness. The story is told of a leader at one of the innumerable rallies who said, "We are here to sing and pray and give money. Some folks say that when you talk about money so much you kill the spirit. That ain't so; when you love Jesus, you got to give."

These financial drives were project oriented. Tangible needs were lifted up, and members made major sacrifices on a one-time basis. Most of the needs centered around the church building and property. The usual fund-raising methods, aside from the regular collection, were special appeals, special assessments, envelope appeals (where each member raised a quota), special programs, dinners, and rallies. Often captains were used to collect quotas that the reverend announced from the pulpit.

In rural communities these special occasions were planned according to the seasons of the farming year, such as Men's Day during pepper season, Mother's Day during strawberry season, Youth Day in June during cucumber season, Women's Day during cotton-picking time (the first pay period for school teachers after the summer break), and the Harvest Rally during the selling of tobacco. Other popular rallies were the King and Queen Rally, the Twelve Tribes Rally, the Twelve Gates Rally, the Fifty States Rally, church auxiliary rallies, and choir rallies.

These events created a great deal of excitement and friendly (sometimes not so friendly) competition among the congregation. Members were involved and would work and plan all year to raise the most money and be crowned king or queen. There were members who wouldn't come to church but "sent their rally money." It was not uncommon for members to hold portions of their regular "dues" for an upcoming rally.

These occasions were filled with pageantry and pomp. They often included special attire; ladies would wear all white or long dresses, men would wear dark suits and bow ties. Sister churches were invited with their choirs to render the music and boost attendance for these special days, with the promise that "when you have your program, we'll come and help you." Each group would march around the table and put its money on the table as choirs sang; there was excitement, the money was counted and the amount announced. Usually, when all the groups had marched around the table, an offering was taken in case someone had been overlooked. Then the grand total was announced, and the reverend would crown the king or queen. The reverend would always bring remarks of appreciation and gratitude and publicly thank all of the people for their efforts. The reverend would raise the expectation, "We'll do better next year," and this was would be affirmed with, "Amen, reverend!"

Auxiliaries in the churches also participated in fund-raising, but their emphasis was local and foreign mission. These groups would adopt families in the church and community and provide moral, spiritual, and financial aid. These groups, too, had rallies and fund-raisers; however, these programs were more subdued and had less pomp and pageantry. One such group, known as the Willing Workers, maintained its own treasury and turned over any surplus to the church at the end of the year. Mission circles such as the Willing Workers were primarily concerned with caring for sick members.

Other patterns of giving are reflected in three ministers' recollections of stewardship patterns:

A minister from Tennessee, who has been preaching for fifty-two years and who is presently the pastor of First Baptist Church, Macon, Georgia, notes,

> We took offerings, and clubs had rallies. People back then could not read; they did not know about tithing. They looked to the preacher for direction, and that was usually in the form of club rallies. We sold fish and chicken dinners and sandwiches to support the church. Remember, Negroes in the eighteenth and nineteenth centuries and the first quarter of the twentieth century were not literate as a race. The Bible was usually read by the preacher.

The Reverend Sidney Locks, whose father was a preacher at the Little Zion Baptist Church in Opelousas, Louisiana, observes,

> My father did emphasize tithing, but there was a lack of faith by the congregation. Giving was a problem because not enough of the people tithed. Therefore, there were at least an annual plate sale and Men's Day and Women's Day rallies.

The Reverend Willie Scarborough, a pastor for sixty-one years and presently the pastor of the Oak Grove and Saint Paul Baptist churches in Newport News, Virginia, recalls,

> My earliest recollection was the "Box Party." A young girl would fix a box of food, and the young men would bid on the boxes in order to share the box of food with the girl. Sometimes you'd spend ten dollars for a sweet potato. The money would go to the church. I also recall picking cotton; it was called the "preacher's money." Maybe he got twenty-five cents. He didn't get it all, but that's what it was called. You know, God's church cannot be supported on pig's feet and dimes. We owe God ten cents out of every dollar. Pastors have done other things because it's hard to get members to tithe. There are five things I have observed about money and the church:
>
> 1. People are bent on giving that one mite.
> 2. Pastors haven't put enough stress on giving, nor given the program.
> 3. Pastors must lead to have people follow.
> 4. Pastors have an obligation to the church.
> 5. There is diminishing respect for the clergy.

At the Goodwin Memorial Baptist Church in Harrisburg, Pennsylvania, the Reverend Lenworth Morrison gave an appeal for the mission offering, called

"The Sacred Dime Offering." Rev. Morrison said, "This concept affirms that the tenth belongs to the Lord." The historical stewardship tenants of the African American Christian church are still alive. There are strong, clear calls by the reverend to give the Lord his tenth. Attitudes and perceptions toward the reverend, though many were negative (and still are), have not greatly diminished the reverend's credibility with the congregation or in the community. It is still expected that "the reverend needs to say a word from the pulpit" and make offertory appeals. Often the reverend's strong leadership makes the difference between success and failure. It was not and is not uncommon for members to say, "Reverend, the members are waiting to hear from you as to how much to give." The reverend was and is the motivator, the chief fund-raiser, the stewardship committee, and the planner. The reverend has to have a plan.

If you want people to give, tell them "what," "how much," and "what the money will be used for"; this was the philosophy of the African Christian church and reverend. As African American Christians developed, purchased land, graduated from brush arbors, and migrated from rural to urban areas, there was a need for more permanent churches. These early congregations were energetic and loved their churches and reverends. They used what they had and were creative and intentional in giving to the church. Though the word *stewardship* was not employed, the concept was implemented. These congregations gave their time, often working long hours at night giving free labor to build and repair the church. Their influence stimulated others to give money and attend church. They gave their talents: cooking, cleaning, singing, and working. They gave their finances, often giving all they had to meet their quotas. They gave themselves; there was nothing these hardworking souls would not do to help get the program over.

Therefore, the tradition of stewardship in the African American Christian church must not be looked upon with disdain, nor with eyes of sympathy and paternalism. Accept this tradition that was creative, unique, and an indigenous experience that was valid and quite successful. African American congregations were—some would argue still are—crisis-oriented, needs-motivated, and project-oriented groups. Thus, each financial drive had a specific goal: buying hymnals, purchasing choir robes, painting the church, buying pews, and so forth.

African American church leaders dealt with the psychology of giving. There were awards for success—recognition. The reverend would call a person's name and ask him or her to stand on Sunday morning. Persons were crowned king and queen, plaques were given, certificates of achievement were lavishly printed and presented at the programs, names were placed in the bulletin, and pictures were taken and placed on the church bulletin board. One church set a goal for paving the parking lot. The following was included in that church's bulletin:

The goal is $27,000. Church officers, deacons, trustees, chairmen of auxiliaries and committees who have not completed their assessment ($100) please do so.

Recognitions will be presented when:

A Disciple raises	$100	Certificate
A Shepherd raises	$200	White Paperweight
A Good Samaritan raises	$300	Black Paperweight
A Leader raises	$500	Plaque

Remember that April 24 is the deadline for monies to be paid in full.

Summary

Contemporary African American Christian churches are in transition regarding the stewardship emphasis for the ongoing operation of the church's ministry. However, some congregations are resisting change from historical patterns that were successful and nurturing. In planning and initiating new or different procedures for giving, the pastor must be aware of the historical giving patterns of the local church. Most congregations will try to follow the lead of the pastor. Developing an effective stewardship program in African American Christian churches can be helped by the following:

1. Clergy committed to intentional stewardship and tithing.
2. An understanding of the financial patterns of the African American church.
3. Teaching and training sessions for all church leaders and for the congregation on an ongoing basis.
4. Commitment by the entire church to "prove the tithe."
5. Provision of the nurturing fellowship of fund-raising through other means.
6. Consistency, conciseness, and faithfulness.
7. Teaching that biblical stewardship is a more excellent way to support the ministry of Christ.
8. Preaching by the reverend on faith, commitment, stewardship, and tithing.
9. The reverend must be a faithful steward and tither.
10. The reverend and the congregation, as individuals, must be faithful, prayerful, and prove God through the tithe.

For Fifty Years: An Interview with Dr. S. A. Raper

Clifford A. Jones, Sr.

Dr. Raper, would you tell us a bit about your early years?

I was born in Oconee County in the state of Georgia. My daddy was a farmer, a cotton farmer. The boll weevils came in 1922 and destroyed the cotton crops in Georgia. We moved to North Carolina in 1923, to Cleveland County. I went to Washington Elementary School from 1923 until 1932. When I finished elementary school, the only high school in Cleveland County was Cleveland High School. There were no buses for the blacks at that time; the whites had buses, but the blacks didn't. So to get a high school education, I walked eight miles to school and eight miles back—a whole year going to high school, eight miles in the rain, sleet, and snow. I was determined I would have a high school education and buy a home; we were tenant farmers, and I didn't want that to be my way of life.

When were you called to preach?

I was called to preach in 1944. I was living in Hartford, Connecticut. I had finished high school, but I needed more training. I came back south to go to college. I went to Western Union Academy because it was the only institute we had that was Baptist. It closed in 1945. Then I went to Friendship Junior College, finishing in 1947. I continued my education at Johnson C. Smith University.

How many churches have you pastored?

I have pastored five churches. The first church I pastored was Maple Springs Baptist Church in Shelby, North Carolina. The next church was Cleveland Chapel in Spartanburg, South Carolina. The next church was Cherryville Baptist Church in Cherryville, North Carolina, and the next church was in Brevard, North Carolina—Bethel "A." Mount Calvary in Shelby, North Carolina, is where I am now.

How long were you at the church in Brevard?

I was at the church in Brevard for fifteen years.

How long have you been at Mount Calvary?

Twenty-five years.

What financial patterns did you find when you went to these churches? How did they raise money?

At each church that I went to, the church was selling, soliciting, and doing anything to get money—selling chicken dinners and ice cream and having raffles.

Why did you become committed to the stewardship of tithing?

Well, I worked at the Cleveland Club for governors O. Max Gardner and Clyde R. Hoey when I was going to high school. They taught me that since I was working at that club and making some money, I should give my tithe. After giving my tithe to the church, I began to grow financially. Then I learned that tithing was the way for Christian giving. At each church I went to, I began to teach the people to tithe. At each church I went to, the people were selling, they were begging, they were soliciting. But after I had been with them some time, praying, training, and teaching, the church stopped selling and soliciting and started tithing.

Was it hard to change these churches from the pattern of dinners, raffles, ice cream, potlucks, and all that? How did you do it?

It was hard to do, but with God all things are possible. I knew this was God's way. I knew this was the Bible way. I stuck with it; and everywhere I've gone, I've taught tithing, nothing but tithing. All the people are not going to tithe. But I learned from the Bible that when two or three come together in God's name, agreeing on the same thing, God will be in their midst (Matthew 8:20). So you have to start with a small group. And as you start with that small group, don't let them do anything else. Then you can get the rest to tithe so that you can carry your program.

What do you teach churches about tithing?

The Bible talks about the tithe and the offering. The tithe means one tenth of everything that comes into your possession, and above that is an offering. So you owe the tithe—you've got to pay that. But you get your blessing through the offering. The more you give above your tithe, the more God will bless you. So, tithing and offering, I teach tithing and offering.

What would you say to pastors who say, "I can't get my folk to tithe"?

I'd just tell them to go back and get on their knees and ask God if they've been converted! I don't believe they're preachers! I don't believe those people in the world who call themselves preachers and don't believe God's Word.

What are some of the things that you teach?

Everywhere I go, I teach the stewardship of tithing. I've been all over the country. I've been to Washington, Texas, California, Georgia, South Carolina, Pennsylvania, New York, Virginia, Washington, D.C.—everywhere. I've been to a lot of churches, teaching tithing.

God is a multiplying God, not an "addition" God, a multiplying God. Addition is too long—two plus two plus two plus two; when you get to ten twos, you'll have twenty. But God is not like that. Multiply! God told Adam to be fruitful and multiply, not add, multiply. This means that five times two is ten, ten times two is twenty. God multiplies! God will give to you so fast that you won't have time to get everything.

So teaching tithing is like this: one grain of corn makes one stalk. One stalk will bring several good ears, and each ear has hundreds of grains. So one grain will bring hundreds of grains. And those grains will bring hundreds of stalks, and so forth. If you were to take one grain of corn and plant it, then harvest and plant, harvest and plant, in seven years you'd have so much corn that the earth would be full of corn.

The same is true with an apple. You can count the seeds in one apple, but you can't count the apples in one seed. One apple has about five good seeds, and those five good seeds will bring five good trees. Those five good trees, if they're fertilized and taken care of, will bring many bushels of apples each year. Spread those apples out and there is no way to count them. That's the way it is with the blessings of God; you can't count them.

And you believe God does the same thing with our money?

Yes, God does the same thing with our money! It has been proven to me! I know what God can do!

How do you help a church change from selling dinners and other forms of fund-raising? What would be the first step for pastors to do to help a church change from that pattern to tithing?

First, pastors must be convinced themselves. If you're convinced and tell the story and tell it long enough and believe it, someone else is going to believe it. The pastor can get the deacons to believe; the pastor can get the missionaries to believe; the pastor can get the Sunday school to believe. When those agencies begin to tithe, then the others come on, and then you have a tithing church.

What part does the pastor play in developing a tithing church?

The pastor plays all the parts, because the pastor has control of the church. Jesus said, "Peter, I give you the keys" (Matthew 16:19, paraphrased). Peter has the keys, not the deacons, not anybody else. The pastor has the keys, and it is left with the pastor to develop that church. With the help of God and with faith, the pastor will have a church that is successful in tithing.

What do you say to people when they say that tithing is only in the Old Testament?

Well, they haven't read the Bible! They need to read! Jesus said, "Woe unto you, scribes and Pharisees, hypocrites! for ye pay tithe of mint and anise and cummin, and have omitted the weightier matters of the law, judgment, mercy, and faith: these ought ye to have done, and not to leave the other undone" (Matthew 23:23, KJV). Jesus said, "Don't leave it undone." My contention is this: if a Pharisee, a hypocrite, tithed, what should a Christian do? If your faith is no greater than that of a Pharisee, you can't see the kingdom of heaven. Now, don't you have enough faith in Christ to believe that if you do what he says, he'll do what he says? The Bible says to tithe, and I believe that it is in the New Testament. If you don't have a penny, you ought to have faith; if you don't have a dime, you ought to have love; if you don't have a quarter, you ought to have mercy. These are the essential things; money is not essential to Christianity, but money helps carry out the work of God in a Christian spirit.

What do you say to a person who says, "I'm willing to tithe, but do I tithe off the gross or the net?"

Now that has been an argument! I believe that you should tithe from your income. "And if a man will at all redeem ought of his tithes, he shall add thereto the fifth part thereof. And concerning the tithe of the herd, or of the flock, even of whatsoever passeth under the rod, the tenth shall be holy unto the Lord" (Leviticus 27:31-32, KJV). If you're working and they take out taxes, your tithe should be based on what you get. If you bring a check home for three hundred dollars, you owe the Lord thirty dollars plus. You can't tithe out of what you don't get. If you bring home one hundred dollars, you owe the Lord ten dollars plus, that's all. When you get old and start drawing on your Social Security, then you pay on that. All that comes under the rod you can give. A lot of people pay from the other part. You can't give God too much; if you paid out of your groceries, it wouldn't be too much. It's all that comes under the rod, and that is in Leviticus.

What would you tell a young couple who says, "We can't afford to tithe"?

Well, if you can't afford to tithe, you can't afford to pay your debts, because you can't pay your debts—prayerfully, hopefully, freely—without tithing. A young married couple buys a home; if they start giving God the tithe, they'll pay for that home. In our church there's a young couple who tithes. They have paid for their home in less than ten years; a fifty-thousand-dollar home, and in less than ten years they have paid for it. They have bought another home, and they'll keep on going. If a young couple tithes, I'll guarantee you they'll pay for everything they've got and have money.

What do you think it means when Malachi says, "I will open up the windows of heaven for you and pour out a blessing" (Malachi 3:10, LB)?

Well, our church has three doors, but it has ten windows. That is to say, the doors are not enough to bring in all that God's going to give you, so you'll have to open the windows. That's God; God does that! God pours it in. You don't know where it's coming from; it comes this way, that way.

When people tithe, will they get only financial blessings?

They'll not only receive financial blessings, they'll receive physical blessings, too! They'll get a happy life! I've been tithing ever since 1933, when I made my first ten dollars. O. Max Gardner said, "Pay your money!" I started tithing, I started giving. I haven't been to the hospital in forty-five years. I haven't been to the doctor except for an examination. I haven't missed a Sunday preaching in the last forty years! God will give you good health, then a good mind, then many friends, then substance. Everything that you need to be happy, God will give to you!

You've been preaching since 1944; you've seen the church change a lot. As you look ahead, what would be your prophecy about the church and stewardship in the twenty-first century?

If black churches give their tithe and do as God says to do, the twenty-first century will be the greatest century that the United States has ever known. Black people who know hardship, who know what God has done for them, don't have to worry about who is president. They don't have to worry about who is governor. They don't have to worry about who is sheriff. The God that we serve is able to take us through, and take the church through!

Is there anything else you want to say about stewardship?

I'd like to tell black preachers all over this country that if they would teach their churches to tithe, if they would teach their churches to do what the Bible says to do, it would be one of the greatest blessings for black people that has ever happened in this country. I know that we have a little church here with less than two hundred members. We haven't solicited! We haven't done anything; everything comes from tithes and offerings. This little church gives as much to the work of Christ as any other church in this vicinity. We never solicit anything! We don't have Men's Day! We don't have Women's Day! We don't have Children's Day! We don't have any kind of program in our church to raise money.

Should the church tithe out of its income?

Yes! Mission! So far, our church has given more than 15 percent for mission. We've given something like 20 percent this year for mission.

Would you recommend that churches tithe for mission from their budgets?

Yes, I would suggest that, at least, churches tithe from their income. If a church takes in two thousand dollars on a Sunday, two hundred dollars or more should go for mission. If a church takes in five thousand dollars, five hundred dollars or more should go for mission. Then the church will prosper.

I hope the day comes (I don't know if I'm going to live that long or not) when this church can pay half of its income for mission. When we get our church paid for and everything settled, I'm going to try to get up to at least 40 percent. If you don't owe anything, that's what you should do. I'd like our church to pay at least 40 percent of our income for mission and education.

Thank you, Dr. Raper. Do you have any closing statements about stewardship, tithing, and the preacher?

Stay with God's Word and you can make it!

A Thriving Church

O. T. Tomes

I have been entrusted with a stewardship. (I Corinthians 9:17, NKJV)

For God has picked me out and given me this sacred trust and I have no choice. (I Corinthians 9:17, LB)

The words of our text reveal the "why" of the sermon. I stand here feeling similar to Paul when he said to the Corinthians, "Do bear with me and let me say what is on my heart" (2 Corinthians 11:1, LB). This is my earnest request to you today. The Lord has entrusted me with a stewardship that I am bound to discharge as your pastor. To this end, I have come to share with you what the Lord has laid on my heart. I will admit at the outset that the subject could very well be misconstrued if one were to examine it with a cynical mind-set. However, my prayer is that you will seek to listen with a spiritual ear and a prayerful mind as we attempt to do three things: review the past, examine the present, and glance with a discerning eye toward the twenty-first century.

A Review of the Past

Twenty years ago you as a community of faith responded to the leading of God's guidance and counsel and invited me to become your pastor. God be thanked! Stony was the road to be trodden as pastor and people, and gloomy was the forecast.

The first two and a half years of our journey were a time of prayerful inventory for me personally. During that period the Lord provided me with many

---

O. T. Tomes is pastor of the New Mount Olive Missionary Baptist Church in Asheville, North Carolina. He is on the board of directors of the Human Service Board of Asheville, North Carolina, and the general board of the General Baptist State Convention. He is active in civic and religious organizations in his area and is a frequent speaker and lecturer.

helpful insights about the spiritual and political climate of the congregation known as the New Mount Olive Missionary Baptist Church. What an insightful experience it was! It was obvious to me that because of decaying spiritual conditions, compounded by a false notion of the importance of spiritual leadership and biblical literacy, there had to be a resurrection if we were going to be the community of faith that God intended us to be. And because a resurrection in my personal life had kept me from going to an early grave, I was persuaded that God could and would do the same for us as a people of faith. To this end we first had to roll away some old stones of tradition and replace them with "foundation stones" that would ensure resurrection in the life and ministry of this congregation. With this resolve, under the caption of "Wholistic Stewardship and Leadership Development," we were led of God to begin the process.

The very first foundation stone was a "training stone." How did Jesus train leaders? A three-fold model emerged:

1. *The Principle of Concentration*
   A few thoroughly trained workers are more effective than many who are superficially trained.

2. *The Principle of Personality*
   A good leader draws out and includes different personalities. This is an essential principle in the training of Christian leaders because it helps leaders develop character.

3. *The Principle of Reality*
   The most important and potent instrument of character training is personal association.

The second foundation stone was a "governmental stone." This was modeled on *God's People and Church Government,* by Robert Lemon.[1] During my time of personal inventory, I came to see that many of the members, who had been good Baptists for a number of years, were totally ignorant of the kind of church government we functioned under as a Missionary Baptist church. Lemon's book helped us examine various forms of church government. It enabled us to clearly understand the kind of government we functioned under as a congregation.

The third stone was the "leadership stone." We built on this foundation with principles and insights gained from *God's Plan for Church Leadership,* by Knofel Staton.[2] As we built on this particular foundation, we discovered that it was an exciting biblical approach to church polity. It required us to honestly examine ourselves and acknowledge the kind of leadership God requires for the church. This particular stone became very painful for a nucleus of our members. It challenged a long-standing tradition of this congregation and finally led to an attempt to terminate my tenure as pastor. Because the two previous stones were already intact, the majority of you as members decided that God's

Word must take precedence over the "traditions of people." Thanks be to God! However, I sincerely believe that this conflict enabled us as a community of faith to examine the fourth stone with a greater degree of sensitivity and understanding.

The fourth foundation stone was the "be-wise stone," modeled on Warren Wiersbe's book *Be Wise*.[3] This stone could very well be called the cornerstone of the foundation. It enabled us, in a very positive way, to clearly understand the difference between human knowledge and God's wisdom. It strengthened both our leadership and stewardship, individually as well as corporately. It helped us focus our calling as Christian stewards as we considered

our calling as Christians,
the Christian message,
the local church,
the Christian ministry,
church discipline,
Christian marriage,
personal priorities,
church order,
the church body,
use of our spiritual gifts,
and Christian stewardship.

An Examination of the Present

By successfully putting in place a solid biblical foundation, we paved the way to move very intentionally toward being stewards who were no longer stagnated, toward being a thriving and exciting group of stewards bound together by a common commitment to the lordship of Jesus Christ. We have begun to see what it means to be committed, consistent, and faithful stewards because we have grown wiser in our concept and understanding of what it means to be the body of Christ.

Throughout its history the church has been called by many names and described in various ways, in biblical terms, in sociological language, and in ecclesiological nomenclature. *Biblically* the church is the body of Christ, the bride of Christ, the fellowship of saints, the called-out society, the temple of God, the house of God, and the kingdom of God. *Sociologically* the church is the community of believers, the congregation, the society of the faithful, and the company of the committed. *Ecclesiologically* it is a church, a temple, a mosque, a meetinghouse, a tabernacle, a cathedral, a basilica, a church house, a synagogue, a chapel, a shrine, and a sanctuary.

For those of us who constitute the New Mount Olive Church family, the church is a community of stewards, a partnership of persons who affirm a mutual stewardship of all the gifts of God: human life, all life, the earth, the fruits of the earth, the abilities that God gives in differing measure to all persons, the time that we are privileged to use, and the portion of eternity that is allotted to us. To view the church in this manner helped us eliminate a lot of myths and traditions that had been sanctified to be of God, when in truth God had nothing to do with them from the beginning. The congregation reflected the concept that leadership development and wholistic stewardship were more than phrases and words. This was being lived out as a lifestyle, in both the personal and corporate life and ministry of the congregation.

This provided us with the opportunity to put in place the Stewardship Commission, which adopted the following purpose statement:

> Realizing that we are stewards of God and not owners of anything, we affirm that stewardship is the responsibility of managing one's whole life unselfishly to the glory of God after accepting Jesus Christ as Lord and Savior.

The Commission also adopted a mission statement:

> To establish a nurturing ministry of wholistic stewardship that will enable fellow members to understand stewardship as a total way of life. To have the ability to obtain feedback; to review the effectiveness of communication through worship, teaching, preaching, and personal application.

Members of this commission spent upward of a year in intense orientation, using a number of resources recommended by the pastor to prepare themselves for a more aggressive year-round church-wide stewardship emphasis. This emphasis embodied the resurrection of new attitudes and a new understanding of what it actually means to be Christian stewards.

Five years before I came here as your pastor, God wrought a very personal resurrection in my life. It forced me to reexamine my life, both as a believing disciple and a steward of the Lord Jesus Christ. This examination led me to embrace what I have termed a wholistic lifestyle.

Before this personal resurrection there was a time when the doctor ordered me to wrap my feet in plastic, put disposable gloves on my hands, and take a pill before retiring to bed. I had to take a blood-pressure pill, which contained three medications, every morning. I was on my way to an early grave. Then I realized that I trusted the same Jesus who called the widow of Nain's son back from the dead. He, too, was on his way to the grave. As a matter of fact, he had already died, and they were rolling him through the gate. I wasn't quite there yet. But I was on my way! Several doctors had warned me that one of two things would happen to me: I would have a massive stroke and become a vegetable, or I would have a heart attack and die a sudden death. I began to think of the compassion Jesus showed the widow of Nain, and about the way that he went forward and touched the funeral bier. The pall bearers stood still, and then the man who had been dead sat up and began to speak. I realized that this same Jesus would touch me.

Like King Hezekiah (2 Kings 20:1-19), I turned my face toward God and vowed that I would become a better steward of the body entrusted to me. I embarked on a fitness program. I am now an avid jogger, averaging thirty-five to forty miles a week. I remember a visit that I had from Deacon McKinley Ellis shortly after coming here as your pastor. He came to the office one day to talk with me about a concern. He shared with me that it was quite embarrassing to him to have "his pastor running around town with his rump showing" (wearing jogging shorts). I assured him that I deeply appreciated him sharing this with me. I also apologized to him for any embarrassment that I had caused him, but I assured him that he would continue to be embarrassed for a long time. I said, "If I stop being intentional about my physical fitness, then I won't be spiritually fit to stand strong in the Lord on Sunday." Thanks be to God who gives us the victory! God granted me a two-fold victory: for more than eighteen years, I've taken no medicine, and my blood pressure is normal. Before Deacon Ellis went home to be with the Lord, he came to the track to walk with me on two different occasions. For the past eight years, the church has conducted an aerobics class three days a week. What a resurrection in attitude on the part of this congregation!

Because of your openness and willingness to become biblically literate, to support and affirm pastoral leadership, to put in place leadership development, and to establish a year-round wholistic stewardship emphasis, the outcome has been unbelievable. Many of you will recall that prior to this you as a congregation were known among other congregations as a stagnant and decaying church. Average Sunday school attendance was 32 with an offering of less than $10 per Sunday. Few young people attended, and those who did often became dropouts (especially the males) by the time they got to junior high school. It was unheard of for high school males to be involved in the life and ministry of this congregation. Even worse, college was a no-no for most of our young men. But what a difference now! Look at the leadership that Jermine Smith, a high school senior, is giving as our assistant superintendent. We have hit an all-time high in Sunday school attendance, averaging 121, with the offering averaging $110 per Sunday.

When I came, the average attendance for Sunday morning worship was 52, mostly senior citizens. Out of a membership of 250, our average worship attendance is now 140. When I came, the total offering on Sunday was usually $86, and if by chance it was $105, it was believed that the Lord had opened the windows of heaven and poured out a blessing. Tithing and sacrificial giving were a no-no in this congregation. Now, doing things God's way, the average Sunday offering is $3,650, with the largest percentage coming from tithes.

As a result of coming to grips with wholistic stewardship as a lifestyle, there are other measurable and tangible results that reflect the life and ministry of this church family. For example, we have joined with the business community to make our Summer Youth Employment Service vital to Asheville businesses. Thanks to the untiring efforts of the Stewardship Commission, thirty-one youth are employed in the business sector of the community. Because of the success of this ministry, businesses and other agencies have invited members of the commission to hold seminars sharing our program's methods. At our recent Stewardship Youth Employment banquet, eleven businesses awarded us plaques in appreciation for being able to employ youth who had gone through our employment orientation program. We also received official commendation from the city of Asheville. In addition to these, twenty-two other active and vibrant ministries are an integral and vital part of this church:

Leadership development
Focused Bible study
Year-round stewardship nurturing
Tutorial classes for all school students
New-member orientation classes for adults and children
Year-round emphasis on African American history
Physical fitness ministry
Music ministry
Counseling (family, individual, marital, premarital)
Marriage enrichment
Youth employment counseling
Radio ministry (Sunday morning live broadcast)
Visitation ministry
Prison outreach (to men and women)
Singles ministry
Mentoring for young black males
Bus ministry
Ministry to the homeless
Asheville Buncombe Christian Community Outreach
Witnessing outreach
Ministry-action teams
Family-life ministry

I praise God and give God the glory for all that he is doing with us and through us. Some of you have remarked to me, "Pastor, God is really blessing us." Our church is a thriving church now. I'll be the first to admit that God is still blessing us. And we cannot yet see what will happen with us and through us if we continue in our faithfulness as God's stewards.

However, I must tell you that all is not well. For every now and then I hear those among us who have found reasons not to commit themselves to the biblical concept of giving say, "Well, I guess you know that this business of tithing is nothing but a con scheme by the pastor to get more money." It distresses me that there are those who allege this biblical concept is a scheme in spite of the fact that God has honored and blessed us so that we could build a new edifice and acquire more land; in spite of the fact that many of the young men and women who grew up in this church did not drop out but went to college and are now working and giving their tithes; in spite of the fact that when I came here you were able to count on one hand, with some room left, the number of families who took vacations; in spite of the fact that a number of you who were living in the Asheville Housing Development— and there is nothing wrong with living there—now own your own home. All of this attests to the fact that stewardship is more than just giving a tithe. It is the direct result of being good stewards of the 90 percent that God leaves in our custody. To hear it said that tithing is a scheme, or an Old Testament law, distresses me, especially when the truth speaks for itself. So be careful to whom you listen!

Many of you, as members, know by now that stewardship is not some form of theoretical gymnastics for me, but a consistent, committed, and applied lifestyle. The same can be said for many of you. But this is not to say that this type of applied lifestyle has been free of stress; it has not. Any time you commit yourself to be one of God's faithful stewards you invite some stressful times along the way. Even my twelve-year-old daughter, Tomara, is aware of this fact. As we were driving to church one Sunday, she asked, "Daddy, what are you preaching about this Sunday? Will it be about stress in the life of a steward?" I responded by saying, "No, I am preaching about unhealthy tensions that will ruin your life as a steward." Dr. J. Alfred Smith, Sr., says, "Pastors who fail, because of fear of criticism or timidity, to systematically teach tithing and stewardship are depriving people of spiritual growth. In fact, these well-meaning pastors are innocently and unintentionally inviting spiritual problems into the lives of those which the Holy Spirit has made them overseers."[4]

A Glance Toward the Future

As we move toward the twenty-first century, we as Christian stewards will have to contend more and more with lifestyles that will be more secular in mind-set than spiritual. More and more pew occupants will opt for faith that is feeling in nature rather than faith that is determined by commitment. Pastors will be bombarded with requests for instantaneous spiritual quick fixes on demand, and if they fail to provide, they will immediately feel the scorn and wrath of the ones making such a request.

As we move toward the twenty-first century, particularly in African American congregations, our commitment to a vital stewardship ministry is imperative. And might I add, it cannot be a ministry that is activated around annual budget time. It must be an ongoing process. We must not be ashamed of teaching, preaching, and modeling a lifestyle of consistent Christian stewardship. Let me close with this poem based on the King James Version of 2 Timothy 1:12. As stewards this must be our badge of confidence:

> I am not ashamed, for I know and am persuaded,
>> A demonstration of confidence.
> I know whom I have believed,
>> A declaration of trust.
> He is able to keep that which I have committed unto him,
>> A deposit of value.
> Against that day!
>> A day of reckoning! For we will give an account
>> of our stewardship before God.

A Pastoral Word
on Stewardship:
Luke 16:10-11

William A. Lawson, Jr.

"He who is faithful in very little is faithful also in much; and he who is dishonest in a very little is dishonest also in much. If then you have not been faithful in the unrighteous mammon, who will entrust to you the true riches?" (Luke 16:10-11)

Not long ago we preached about money. We urged Christians to give the first tenth of their income to God, and we reminded them of Malachi's prophecy that promised that God would bless tithers beyond their ability to receive (Malachi 3:10). Using fruits and vegetables, Dr. Wyatt Tee Walker illustrated how little God asks of us and how much we are allowed to keep for ourselves; we saw God's one-tenth in a little stack on a flower pedestal and our nine-tenths piled high and overflowing on to the floor. It's time to talk about money again.

Money is a highly charged subject, and people are extremely sensitive about it. Television stars, athletes, or executives have been our heroes—until they got into a salary conflict. Then their image was tarnished, their status as heroes bruised. Perhaps you can remember someone who was a good friend of yours—until you lost your job and needed money. Then the friendship faded

William A. Lawson, Jr., is pastor of the Wheeler Avenue Baptist Church in Houston, Texas. He has been active in civic affairs, civil rights, and character-building programs in Houston for many years and was recently appointed to the board of the Texas Department of Mental Health and Mental Retardation.

away. Or perhaps there was a person you liked—until they failed to repay a debt to you and began to lie to you and avoid you. That relationship was permanently damaged; it may never again be the same. Perhaps you have known people from another country and thought that they were great people—until they began to badger you to finance them, to sign as their guarantor, or to help them bring their children, mates, or relatives to the United States. Then you didn't want to talk to them on the phone.

Money is very close to our hearts. It is the first thing we want to know about when we consider a job. It is impolite to admit this, so we never ask about it first; but it is really what we want to know first. George Bush failed to be reelected not because of the conflict with Iraq but because we held him responsible for the failure of the United States' economy. He couldn't bring back the money days. In fact, the main reason for interest in Ross Perot was not dissatisfaction with the two parties but the thought that this aggressive billionaire could turn our economy around. He was the only candidate identified with a financial label, "billionaire Ross Perot."

Money matters so much that we will endure a lot of pain to get it. People will live with a person who drinks too much, who uses drugs, or who cheats on them—because the money is good. But when that person ceases to produce consistently good money, he or she is history. Social workers, counselors, and law enforcement people have never been able to explain to me why victims of abuse will stay with a "pimp type" except to say that the need for financial security is greater than the need for self-esteem. How much abuse will a person take for a great wardrobe and a Seville?

So when a preacher talks about money, people tune that preacher out. But this simply means that they do not know what the Bible is all about. Money is the measuring stick Jesus most often used in his parables about human nature: the unjust steward, the parable of the talents, the parable of the rich man's barns, the parable of the rich man and Lazarus, the parable of the lost sheep, the parable of the lost coin, the parable of the lost son. These parables address the way that people deal with money or property. And you could go on to list many of Jesus' metaphors, such as the rich man and the eye of a needle, the lilies of the field that neither toil nor spin, and the comment that foxes have holes and birds have nests, but the Son of man is homeless.

Your money says more about you than almost anything else. There is an inverse relationship between money and people. The less you value people, the more you value money; the more you value people, the less you value money. Perhaps the most powerful words Jesus used about money were, "Where your treasure is, there will your heart be also" (Luke 12:34).

In Luke 16:1-9 Jesus told a story about an unscrupulous servant. Knowing that he was about to be fired for poor management, this servant won friends from among his master's debtors by reducing the amounts they owed the master. Yet, Jesus said that this dishonest servant understood the real value of money better than religious people do. Jesus followed this story with our text (Luke 16:10-11), urging us to understand that money is tied to our faith. If we cannot show our faith by the way we handle money, why should God turn the riches of salvation over to us? Eternal life is a much bigger treasure than earthly dollars.

Why do preachers talk about money? Is it to be sure our salaries are paid? Is it to keep our churches financed? Are our words just commercials to make sure that customers buy our product? This would certainly be an obvious reason. But it would not explain why Sunday school teachers or unpaid pew members talk about money. It would not explain why my parents or yours were such stubborn tithers, even when they were mad at the preacher or felt neglected by the church. It would not explain why children's workers demand that children, who have only pennies, bring an offering to God—even when they want to use their little money at McDonald's or Burger King. These workers in Sunday school, in children's church, and in vacation Bible school are not paid for what they teach; in fact, their teaching is a form of giving.

What, then, is so important that we keep twisting your arm to give cheerfully to God? Quite simply, in giving you commit to God what is most precious to you, and God in return blesses you. We see this in Scripture in the story of Abraham and Isaac, the story of Elijah and the widow of Zarephath, and the stories of Daniel and Shadrach, Meshach, and Abednego.

God promised Abraham that he and his wife, Sarah, would have a son. This seemed impossible to Abraham and Sarah, but in time God gave them a son, Isaac. What could have been more precious to Abraham than Isaac? Yet, to test the depths of Abraham's faith, God asked Abraham to sacrifice Isaac—to give Isaac back to God. Abraham responded in faith, willing to give what he valued most to God. And God responded, "Because you have done this, . . . I will indeed bless you" (Genesis 22:16-17).

It was a time of drought, and the widow of Zarephath was down to her last handful of grain when Elijah asked her for food. This small amount was all that stood between the widow and her son and death. It had great value for her. Yet, Elijah asked her to share it with him. In return, Elijah promised that God would continue to provide food for her family until the drought ended. Scripture tells us that "she went and did as Elijah said; and she, and he, and her household ate for many days" (1 Kings 17:15).

For Daniel and Shadrach, Meshach, and Abednego, commitment to God meant refusing the food and wine of Nebuchadnezzar. The food and the wine were the best that Babylon had to offer. But they were "unclean" by Hebrew standards. Daniel and the others chose to honor God. And God blessed them so that "in every matter of wisdom and understanding concerning which the king inquired of them, he found them ten times better than all the magicians and enchanters that were in all his kingdom" (Daniel 1:20).

You can't get a guarantee that God will bless you—you have to go out in faith. Joshua, Caleb, and the other spies all saw the perils present in the land that God had promised Israel (Numbers 13). In their fear and disbelief, most of the spies and the people of Israel chose to remain in the wilderness. Only Joshua and Caleb believed enough to act (Numbers 14). Only Joshua and Caleb would enter the Promised Land. You can't get a guarantee that God will bless you. But if you sanctify your paycheck and give God the first fruits of it, God will pour out a blessing too great for you to contain.

We relate to the world by experience. We relate to God by faith. We know God has already taken care of us. We know that God will not let us fall. We are like the baby whose daddy throws her in the air and gently catches her each time. At first we are a little bit frightened, but soon we come to know that we will not be dropped. Then, we shout with joy as we are thrown skyward, confident that strong arms will not let us fall.

The opening of the 1992 Summer Olympics was a lavish spectacle, with athletes from nations around the world marching together into the stadium in Barcelona, Spain. One of the poorer of the European countries, Spain spent the equivalent of nine billion dollars to host the Olympics because Spain was committed to this athletic event. Spain did not expect to receive gold medals. The honor of hosting this event, the satisfaction of supporting the Olympic movement, and the respect of the world community were Spain's rewards.

How much, then, should Christians give to God? How much is God worth? God sent his Son, Jesus Christ, to pay a price greater than ten trainloads of gold medals. How much more is God worth? God does not leave you impoverished after you give, but returns what you commit—pressed down, shaken together, and running over.

All Scripture quotations in this sermon are from the Revised Standard Version of the Bible unless otherwise noted.

Developing Christian Stewards Through Tithing: A Lesson

Clifford A. Jones, Sr.

The purpose of this lesson

This lesson is intended to enhance the knowledge of Christian stewards about the biblical principle of tithing and to affirm that stewards are ultimately accountable to God.

The limitations of this lesson

This lesson is designed to be taught in one or two fifty-minute sessions during Sunday school, new member orientation classes, deacon's or trustee's meetings, retreats, or seminars. Selected Scriptures establish the biblical basis for tithing.

The goal of this lesson

The goal of this lesson is for Christian stewards to commit themselves to the biblical principle of tithing.

Introduction

A Christian acknowledges through faith that Jesus is the Christ, the unique Son of God; that he lived, suffered under Pontius Pilate, was crucified, buried, raised from the dead, ascended into heaven, and presently intercedes for the church. "The word is near you, on your lips and in your heart (that is, the word of faith which we preach); because, if you confess with your lips that Jesus is Lord and believe in your heart that God raised him from the dead, you will be saved" (Romans 10:8-9).

Having responded to divine initiative, Christians now must live from the foundation of divine will as it was demonstrated in the life of Jesus. This is accomplished by actively surrendering our will, priorities, and agenda to the will of the Divine for our lives. Led by the empowering of the Holy Spirit, Christians are continuously surrendering as God's Spirit teaches them and elevates their consciousness. Listen to our Lord as he speaks to the disciples: "These things I have spoken to you, while I am still with you. But the Counselor, the Holy Spirit, whom the Father will send in my name, he will teach you all things, and bring to your remembrance all that I have said to you" (John 14:25-26).

Through faith the Christian lives in a unique relationship with the Divine and is granted spiritual power for daily experiences. However, there are moments when we succumb to our human frailty and live beneath our Christian dignity. There are moments when we claim ownership of our destiny. There are times when we are callous and cold in the presence of imminent need, in circumstances that call for our love and action. Yet, we are content in the serenity of pseudosaintliness. We sin! However, the Christian cannot adopt a defeatist moral, emotional, and spiritual posture. The same God who provided for our initial relationship also provides for our forgiveness. We must continually confess our sins in Jesus' name: "If we say we have no sin, we deceive ourselves, and the truth is not in us. If we confess our sins, he is faithful and just, and will forgive our sins and cleanse us from all unrighteousness. If we say we have not sinned, we make him a liar, and his word is not in us" (1 John 1:8-10).

God in Jesus Christ has adequately provided for our present and eternal destiny. Being Christian stewards, living under the auspices of divine favor, we must respond in faith—a faith that is functional and practical, a faith that reaches to the utmost parts of the world developing Christian stewards through tithing.

What it means to be a steward

The Old Testament concept of a steward was that of a person who manages affairs, oversees services, and directs the organizational structure on behalf of the owner. Thus, stewardship involved management, and the steward was ultimately accountable and responsible to the owner. The following Scripture passages reflect this understanding of both *steward* and *stewardship:*

This proposal seemed good to Pharaoh and to all his servants. And Pharaoh said to his servants, "Can we find such a man as this, in whom is the Spirit of God?" So Pharaoh said to Joseph, "Since God has shown you all this, there is none so discreet and wise as you are; you shall be over my house, and all my people shall order themselves as you command; only as regards the throne will I be greater than you." And Pharaoh said to Joseph, "Behold, I have set you over all the land of Egypt." Then Pharaoh took his signet ring from his hand and put it on Joseph's hand, and arrayed him in garments of fine linen, and put a gold chain about his neck; and he made him to ride in his second chariot; and they cried before him, "Bow the knee!" Thus he set him over all the land of Egypt (Genesis 41:37-43).

Observations:

1. A steward is guided by the Spirit of God (v. 38).
2. A steward is discreet and wise (v. 39).
3. A steward is given authority and is responsible and accountable (v. 40).

Then he commanded the steward of his house, "Fill the men's sacks with food, as much as they can carry, and put each man's money in the mouth of his sack, and put my cup, the silver cup, in the mouth of the sack of the youngest, with his money for the grain." And he did as Joseph told him. As soon as the morning was light, the men were sent away with their asses. When they had gone but a short distance from the city, Joseph said to his steward, "Up, follow after the men; and when you overtake them, say to them, 'Why have you returned evil for good? Why have you stolen my silver cup? Is it not from this that my lord drinks, and by this that he divines? You have done wrong in so doing' " (Genesis 44:1-5).

Observations:

1. A steward is under the direct command and auspices of a ruler (v. 1).
2. A steward is required to be obedient (v. 4).
3. A steward is to carry the master's message (v. 4).

These Scripture passages identify three major characteristics of a steward:

1. The steward is given specific duties and responsibilities by the owner or ruler.
2. The steward is a servant of the owner or ruler.
3. The steward is not the owner, nor does the steward function autonomously.

An understanding of a steward in relationship to God as owner and ruler involves time, talents, possessions, influence, and self; all that a steward is, is a direct result of God's goodness, and all that a steward has is a direct result of God's blessings. It is God's will for stewards to be managers of a portion of God's estate. We are recipients and partakers of divine mercy and goodness. Ultimate sovereignty and ownership belong unequivocally to God. Consequently, stewards are accountable to God and responsible for how equitably they manage the time, talents, possessions, influence, and *imago dei* that God has entrusted to them. Stewards are caretakers of divine resources; everything belongs to God. This is clearly amplified in Psalm 24:1-2:

> The earth is the Lord's and the fulness thereof,
>   the world and those who dwell therein;
> for he has founded it upon the seas,
>   and established it upon the rivers.

A New Testament concept of *steward* must include the teachings of Jesus, the Christ. He was a master teacher who sought to enhance understanding of divine truth. Jesus said that it is essential to understand whose we are and to use the things entrusted to us for the kingdom of God—specifically as it relates to the poor, the weak, the disabled, the elderly, the powerless, the children, the hungry, and the spiritually dead. The divine kingdom is actualized in our midst. Stewards ought at least to provide opportunities for heavenly manna to be tasted on earth.

In Christendom, Jesus, the Christ, is God's purest and fullest revelation of love, grace, and truth: "And the Word became flesh and dwelt among us, full of grace and truth; we have beheld his glory, glory as of the only Son from the Father" (John 1:14). Jesus sternly condemned pseudoreligious classism, pernicious actions, and fashionable pray-ers who enjoyed lofty praise from their peers while willfully and systematically denying, ignoring, and overlooking those who had less. However, our Lord did not condemn wealth; he did condemn the steward who acted as owner and denied his sisters and brothers in need (Luke 12:42-47). Two examples of Jesus' teachings follow:

And he said to them, "Take heed, and beware of all covetousness; for a man's life does not consist in the abundance of his possessions." And he told them a parable, saying, "The land of a rich man brought forth plentifully; and he thought to himself, 'What shall I do, for I have nowhere to store my crops?' And he said, 'I will do this: I will pull down my barns, and build larger ones; and there I will store all my grain and my goods. And I will say to my soul, Soul, you have ample goods laid up for many years; take your ease, eat, drink, be merry.' But God said to him, 'Fool! This night your soul is required of you; and the things you have prepared, whose will they be?' So is he who lays up treasure for himself, and is not rich toward God."

And he said to his disciples, "Therefore I tell you, do not be anxious about your life, what you shall eat, nor about your body, what you shall put on. For life is more than food, and the body more than clothing. Consider the ravens: they neither sow nor reap, they have neither storehouse nor barn, and yet God feeds them. Of how much more value are you than the birds! And which of you by being anxious can add a cubit to his span of life? If then you are not able to do as small a thing as that, why are you anxious about the rest? Consider the lilies, how they grow; they neither toil nor spin; yet I tell you, even Solomon in all his glory was not arrayed like one of these. But if God so clothes the grass which is alive in the field today and tomorrow is thrown into the oven, how much more will he clothe you, O men of little faith! And do not seek what you are to eat and what you are to drink, nor be of anxious mind. For all the nations of the world seek these things; and your Father knows that you need them. Instead, seek his kingdom, and these things shall be yours as well.

"Fear not, little flock, for it is your Father's good pleasure to give you the kingdom. Sell your possessions, and give alms; provide yourselves with purses that do not grow old, with a treasure in the heavens that does not fail, where no thief approaches and no moth destroys. For where your treasure is, there will your heart be also" (Luke 12:15-34).

Observations:

1. The quality of life does not reside in the quantity of things.
2. One can be deceived by the personal possessive pronoun *my*.
3. The foolish fail to realize one's ultimate accountability to God.
4. Personal riches can distort perceptions of divine accountability.
5. One needs to place possessions in perspective to life.
6. The divine Creator of the universe provides.
7. The faithful, of necessity, must seek the kingdom and trust God's goodness and mercy.
8. The faithful steward allows the heart, not the treasure, to guide motives and attitudes.
9. The divine prosperity plan requires seeking the kingdom of God and God's righteousness.

Peter said, "Lord, are you telling this parable for us or for all?" And the Lord said, "Who then is the faithful and wise steward, whom his master will set over his household, to give them their portion of food at the proper time? Blessed is that servant whom his master when he comes will find so doing. Truly, I say to you, he will set him over all his possessions. But if that servant says to himself, 'My master is delayed in coming,' and begins to beat the menservants and the maidservants, and to eat and drink and get drunk, the master of that servant will come on a day when he does not expect him and at an hour he does not know, and will punish him, and put him with the unfaithful. And that servant who knew his master's will, but did not make ready or act according to his will, shall receive a severe beating. But he who did not know, and did what deserved a beating, shall receive a light beating. Every one to whom much is given, of him will much be required; and of him to whom men commit much they will demand the more" (Luke 12:41-48).

Observations:

1. The teaching of Jesus about stewards was not just for the first-century disciples.

2. The steward was given specific responsibility over the master's possessions.
3. The steward abused the trust and intention of the master through deliberate inequities and injustices.
4. The master held the steward accountable.
5. The owner treated the steward with reciprocity: as the steward acted, so the master acted toward the steward.

> He also said to the disciples, "There was a rich man who had a steward, and charges were brought to him that this man was wasting his goods. And he called him and said to him, 'What is this that I hear about you? Turn in the account of your stewardship, for you can no longer be steward.' And the steward said to himself, 'What shall I do, since my master is taking the stewardship away from me? I am not strong enough to dig, and I am ashamed to beg. I have decided what to do, so that people may receive me into their houses when I am put out of the stewardship.' So, summoning his master's debtors one by one, he said to the first, 'How much do you owe my master?' He said, 'A hundred measures of oil.' And he said to him, 'Take your bill, and sit down quickly and write fifty.' Then he said to another, 'And how much do you owe?' He said, 'A hundred measures of wheat.' He said to him, 'Take your bill, and write eighty.' The master commended the dishonest steward for his shrewdness; for the sons of this world are more shrewd in dealing with their own generation than the sons of light. And I tell you, make friends for yourselves by means of unrighteous mammon, so that when it fails they may receive you into the eternal habitations.
>
> "He who is faithful in a very little is faithful also in much; and he who is dishonest in a very little is dishonest also in much. If then you have not been faithful in the unrighteous mammon, who will entrust to you the true riches? And if you have not been faithful in that which is another's, who will give you that which is your own? No servant can serve two masters; for either he will hate the one and love the other, or he will be devoted to the one and despise the other. You cannot serve God and mammon" (Luke 16:1-13).

Observations:

1. The steward's management does not go unrecognized by the owner.
2. The owner reserves the right to call the steward to account at will.
3. The steward who mismanaged the owner's goods also failed to provide for his own future.
4. The steward who is dishonest will be dishonest with a lot or little.
5. The steward must choose a master.

Jesus taught that when people are entrusted with much, much is required of them. As you are blessed with much, much is expected of you in facilitating the kingdom of God. Stewards are accountable to God for their use of the resources entrusted to them; yet, they are given the freedom to invest, spend, share, and keep them. Freedom carries with it responsibility for decisions about the use of the owner's goods. Stewards are responsible for the results that will determine whether they will be found faithful or unfaithful. God ultimately is the owner of all that was, is, and shall be. As stewards of God's trust, we will be judged for how we live, give, and serve God.

The Tithe

To tithe is to give one-tenth of your time, talent, substance, self, and influence for the support and growth of God's kingdom on earth. The tithe is brought and given to God through the local synagogue, mosque, or church where membership is held. The faithful steward acknowledges divine ownership through tithing as a minimum response.

Tithing was an ancient and widespread practice; there are references to tithing in Judaism, Christianity, and other world religions. Old Testament references to tithing reflect the different customs of various historical periods. The New Testament concept of tithing is based on Old Testament principles. However, in the New Testament, attitude and motive become integral aspects of tithing. It has been conjectured that tithing was related to the support of royal sanctuaries, and the tithe was paid to the king or priest. Genesis 14 acknowledges payment of tithes to Melchizedek by Abraham. In the following passage, tithing is connected with the spoils taken in war. Notice carefully the references to tithing:

And Melchizedek king of Salem brought out bread and wine; he was priest of God Most High. And he blessed him and said,
> "Blessed be Abram by God Most High,
>   maker of heaven and earth;
> and blessed be God Most High,
>   who has delivered your enemies into your hand!"
> —Genesis 14:18-20

Observations:

1. Melchizedek was a king and priest of God.
2. He blessed Abram and thanked God for Abram's victory in battle.
3. Abram gave Melchizedek an unsolicited tenth—a tithe.

But you shall seek the place which the Lord your God will choose out of all your tribes to put his name and make his habitation there; thither you shall go, and thither you shall bring your burnt offerings and your sacrifices, your tithes and the offering that you present, your votive offerings, your freewill offerings, and the firstlings of your herd and of your flock; and there you shall eat before the Lord your God, and you shall rejoice, you and your households, in all that you undertake, in which the Lord your God has blessed you (Deuteronomy 12:5-7).

Observations:

1. The tithe was to be brought to a designated place.
2. It was a joyous occasion when God's children came with tithes.
3. The tithe—tenth—was not the maximum gift; offerings were also given.
4. The tithe—tenth—was given to God through the priest; it was a privileged obligation for the giver to affirm divine ownership.

"For I the Lord do not change; therefore you, O sons of Jacob, are not consumed. From the days of your fathers you have turned aside from my statutes and have not kept them. Return to me, and I will return to you, says the Lord of hosts. But you say, 'How shall we return?' Will man rob God? Yet you are robbing me. But you say, 'How are we robbing thee?' In your tithes and offerings. You are cursed with a curse, for you are robbing me; the whole nation of you. Bring the full tithes into the storehouse, that there may be food in my house; and thereby put me to the test, says the Lord of hosts, if I will not open the windows of heaven for you and pour down for you an overflowing blessing. I will rebuke the devourer for you, so that it will not destroy the fruits of your soil; and your vine in the field shall not fail to bear, says the Lord of hosts. Then all nations will call you blessed, for you will be a land of delight, says the Lord of hosts" (Malachi 3:6-12).

Observations:

1. During the time of prosperity, the children of God became slack in giving tithes and offerings.
2. Because they failed to be responsible stewards, the temple was neglected.
3. Divine presence was associated with the temple.
4. God observed those who brought tithes and offerings.
5. A divine appeal was made for recommitment to tithing.
6. Failure to bring tithes and offerings was considered robbery.
7. There is a promise of unmeasurable blessings and prosperity for those who recognize divine ownership through tithing.

Some have said, "Jesus never taught tithing." However, the Gospels reveal that Jesus did not denounce the Old Testament principle of stewardship through tithing. The Gospel of Matthew records Jesus saying, "Think not that I have come to abolish the law and the prophets; I have come not to abolish them but to fulfil them" (Matthew 5:17). Jesus expanded the principle of tithing to include motive, attitude, and treatment of one's neighbor: "So if you are offering your gift at the altar, and there remember that your brother has something against you, leave your gift there before the altar and go; first be reconciled to your brother, and then come and offer your gift" (Matthew 5:23-24). Jesus did not abolish the laws and ordinances of the Old Testament, but expanded them to include acts and attitudes, principle and practice, and mission and motive. This is demonstrated in the following Scripture passages:

"Woe to you, scribes and Pharisees, hypocrites! for you tithe mint and dill and cummin, and have neglected the weightier matters of the law, justice and mercy and faith; these you ought to have done, without neglecting the others. You blind guides, straining out a gnat and swallowing a camel!" (Matthew 23:23-24).

Observations:

1. There is a stern warning against hypocrisy among religious leaders.
2. Tithing was practiced legalistically even to the smallest of possessions.
3. There are practices in the Christian faith that are more important than tithing.
4. In addition to tithing, the steward is expected to practice equity.
5. Stewards can be deceived by their own perception of personal holiness.

"But woe to you Pharisees! for you tithe mint and rue and every herb, and neglect justice and the love of God; these you ought to have done, without neglecting the others" (Luke 11:42).

Observations:

1. Jesus condemned the practice of giving only the tithe; giving a tenth of things is not adequate.
2. One's actions based on the principle of love validate tithing.
3. For Christian stewards it is not either principle or active love, but both.

Summary

The goal of this lesson is for Christian stewards to commit themselves to the biblical principle of tithing. As Christians and members of a Christian church, we need to practice our faith in accordance to Scripture, the Holy Spirit, and church policy. Any policy that a local church establishes should be biblically based, and the support for ministry, mission, building maintenance, and new construction should come from the biblical way, tithing. Not raffles! Not pretty-baby contests! Not dinners! Christians who are committed to Christ as Savior and Lord are to give the tithe to God through the church where their membership is maintained. The tithe should not be divided and given as professional dues, nor forwarded to televangelists, radio pastors, or auxiliary presidents. As often as income is received, the whole tithe should be brought (or directly drafted from your bank account) to God.

During the early part of the twentieth century, there was a fraudulent practice in the rural South known as tenant farming. Negroes, as we were then called, lived on the land of a slave-minded person who promised us half of the profits from the crops we raised, after all expenditures had been deducted. There was no written contractual agreement; it was a "gentlemen's agreement." Invariably, year after year, the owner of the land, after making all the deductions, would end up with all of the profits, and the tenants would end up with nothing for their labor. Could it be that Christian stewards carry on a fraudulent tenant relationship with God, abusing God's trust? Could it be that after all our deductions the portion that is legally and morally God's is gone? And then we say, "Maybe next year we'll have a better crop." Will a person rob God?

A young lady had recently completed new member orientation classes, and the minister inquired how she was doing. After receiving a favorable response, the pastor asked if she "was a tither." With a beautiful, warm smile she said, "No, you told us we didn't have to start off tithing, you let us off easy; you said we could start by giving a portion and grow to tithing. I'm still growing." A Christian steward is to start by giving the tithe—a tenth. Yet, there is more; the tither as a Christian steward of integrity must also practice love, justice, and mercy with all of God's children.

Many of us have found that a Christian steward cannot afford not to tithe. We become recipients of divine reciprocity once all that we are and have has been surrendered to God's power. Many Christians have never been blessed because they have refused to put God and the Word to the test by tithing. Prove God, and see if the windows of heaven won't be opened and awesome blessings come your way. Our sincere prayers are with you as you accept the challenge to become a committed steward through the biblical principle of tithing.

> Trust in the LORD, and do good;
>   so you will dwell in the land, and
>   enjoy security.
>
> Take delight in the LORD,
>   and he will give you the desires of
>   your heart.
>   —Psalm 37:3-4

All Scripture quotations in this lesson are from the Revised Standard Version of the Bible unless otherwise noted.

Call to Commitment:
A Program of Personal
and Church Renewal

This "Call to Commitment" stewardship resource (copyright 1990, World Mission Support, American Baptist Churches in the U.S.A.) is an adaptation of the original "Call to Commitment" stewardship materials produced by World Mission Support, American Baptist Churches in the U.S.A., in 1979. The original material has been totally revised, adapted, and tested for use in African American congregations. The principal test church was Friendship Baptist Church, Charlotte, North Carolina, Dr. Clifford Jones, Sr., pastor.

A task force on stewardship in black congregations created this resource. Task force members were Dr. William Thurmond (chair); Dr. Alfloyd Butler; Dr. Jacob Chatman; the Reverend Lee Jefferson; Dr. Clifford A. Jones, Sr.; Dr. Arthur Manning; Dr. Earl Miller; Dr. Milton Owens, Jr.; and the Reverend O. T. Tomes.

Staff support was provided by the Reverend O. John Eldred, Dr. Richard Rusbuldt, and the Reverend James Widmer.

A Word to Pastors

Would you like to see a church in which people give not to receive special honor or recognition but because they are committed to the gospel of the Lord?

Do you ever wish the church could spend more of its energy not in fundraising but in doing ministry?

Do you dream of having a congregation motivated to support the ministry of the church because they are Christ's disciples, not because they fear being embarrassed when the list of givers is published?

Does your heart yearn for a congregation that has an expanding vision for ministry and at the same time is growing in its ability to provide the leadership and financial resources to carry out that mission?

Do you live in the hope that more of your people will share a worthy portion of their lives, including a tithe (or more) of their financial resources, because that is part of what it means to be Christian?

Would you like to move your church away from simply fund-raising and into the development of Christian stewardship?

If you answered yes to any of these questions, then this ministry of stewardship can help you!

"Call to Commitment" is a ministry of stewardship that is usable in any setting, but the primary focus is stewardship development in the context of the African American Christian traditions. This guide will help pastors lead congregations to a stronger basis of biblical stewardship over a period of four years.

Why use "Call to Commitment"?

1. Discipling Christians involves the growth of stewards. "Call to Commitment" will help develop disciples because its aim is to grow stewards. "Whoever of you does not renounce all that [you have] cannot be my disciple" (Luke 14:33, RSV).
2. It brings a renewed sense of call to follow Christ. The call to Christian commitment is not "once in a lifetime"; it comes to the believer again and again. The church must help that happen!
3. It encourages the declaration of Christ's call for growing commitment to those who are not attending regularly, as well as to those who are present week to week.
4. It provides learning and growing experiences in biblical stewardship year round.
5. It incorporates biblical stewardship into the total life of congregations.
6. It works! Pastors of churches in urban and rural settings with small, medium, or large congregations have used this kind of stewardship ministry with remarkable results. Laity have grown and developed as stewarding disciples in all of life. The vision for ministry and the scope of understanding our global mission as Christians have evolved. Leadership and financial resources have grown accordingly. Budgets have doubled in five years, even tripled in eight years.

The keys are persistence over several years, strong pastoral leadership, and involvement of the creativity of both pastor and laity.

Outline of "Call to Commitment"
A Four-Year Cycle

The development of Christian stewards requires a sustained effort over several years. There is no "quick fix." It requires major changes in attitude, value systems, lifestyle, and behavior patterns in the entire congregation. That takes time. This outline suggests a four-year cycle, which can be repeated for another four years. God doesn't grow a strong oak tree in a year or two. Nor does God grow a congregation of responsible Christian stewards in one or two years! Both are the result of persistent and consistent care and attention.

I. Year One—"Christ's Ministry Through Our Church"

  A. Initial launch of "Call to Commitment"—How to get started

    1. Preparation

      a. The pastor must convince church leaders to give themselves and their support for this multiyear development of biblical stewardship. This "convincing" process should begin many months before you hope to launch "Call to Commitment." The pastor should be familiar with this guide before proposing this stewardship ministry to church leaders.

      b. The pastor should then select and appoint a chairperson. Choose a layperson whose leadership is respected by the church.

      c. The pastor, in consultation with the chairperson, should select and/or convene the stewardship committee.

      d. The pastor should present the outline of "Call to Commitment" to the stewardship committee and secure its promise of wholehearted support. Whether this is a committee already in place or a new committee created to lead "Call to Commitment," the total commitment of all the committee members to this ministry is vital.

      e. The pastor and the committee should develop an adequate and clear time line. It takes three months of planning before launching this ministry in the congregation. Give the launch a prominent place in the calendar and life of the church.

      f. The pastor and chairperson should outline and describe the expectations for each member of the committee. Assign appropriate responsibilities with clear lines of authority and accountability. Before any committee session concludes, set forth who is going to do what by when.

      g. The pastor and committee should customize the design of "Call to Commitment" to fit the unique needs and personality of their congregation.

    2. Launch Month

      a. Set aside an entire month, four consecutive Sundays. Some churches may choose to use five consecutive Sundays.

      b. It is appropriate to start with a Communion service. We are asking people to renew their commitment to Christ, and Communion symbolizes this renewal.

      c. The primary focus of the month is "Christ's Ministry Through Our Church."

d. The pastor and stewardship committee should select an overall theme for the month. Use every means possible to proclaim that theme—words, artwork, video, music, drama, and so on.

e. Center the Sunday morning worship service, and other all-church services, around a weekly emphasis during Launch Month. (See page 157 for example.) Select a monthly theme and weekly emphases that address the needs and concerns of *your* congregation. Each week the pastor must give strong support to the weekly emphasis from the pulpit. This includes the sermon.

f. Use a personal covenant, to be signed by each member, to challenge every person to a month of special study, learning, growth, and commitment to Christ. (See the sample on pages 162-163.)

g. Plan carefully to make members aware of the ministry being done within the congregation for the church family. In presenting "We Have This Ministry," be creative, visual, dramatic! Most people in most congregations have little understanding of the ways that the needs of the members are being served by the church.

h. Clearly lift up the opportunities, the "New Possibilities," open to the church if each member makes a renewed and deeper commitment to Christ. Be very specific. Be excited. Be enthusiastic. Use visual aids whenever possible. Enlist people who are good communicators.

i. The pastor and the stewardship committee need to prepare the church to participate in Prove-the-Tithe Sunday—the third Sunday of Launch Month.

j. Develop a clear picture of "Hopes and Dreams" for next year's ministry. Present this to the congregation on the Sunday the members are asked to make their commitment, to "declare their intention."

k. The final Sunday of Launch Month is Commitment Sunday. Each member of the church should bring his or her declaration of intention to the altar for a prayer of dedication.

l. During the two weeks following Commitment Sunday, those not present on Commitment Sunday should be visited in their homes by trained visitors. It is important to draw these people into the ministry of the church. The deacons should form the core of the visitors to demonstrate their solidarity for this stewardship ministry.

3. Following Commitment Sunday

a. Send a personal letter thanking each person who made a commitment.

b. Complete all home visits within two weeks, and make a final report to the congregation.

c. Celebrate the growth and accomplishments that have taken place. This could include a dinner at the church or a worship service of celebration including Communion. Personal testimonies of growth and development could be shared.

d. It is very important that the church promptly implement plans to use the skills and abilities that have been offered by the members. It is better not to ask for them if you don't plan to use them.

B. The remainder of Year One

1. Continue to select a monthly theme that will maintain the attention of the congregation on growing as stewards. We are to be stewards every day, all year long!

2. The monthly theme needs a weekly focus with specific challenges to grow. These could be a Scripture passage shared in the Sunday school, references in the pastor's sermon, a prayer or other part in the worship service, a testimony from a layperson, or an item in the church bulletin or newsletter. Brief progress reports from the pastor and other people in the congregation on ministries of the church will keep the growth and excitement alive.

3. Provide quarterly progress reports to each person who made a financial commitment.

4. The stewardship committee should meet monthly during the rest of the year to work with the pastor to plan and carry out the monthly events. The committee should also evaluate the effectiveness of each element in the program and begin planning for Year Two. Additional persons should be recruited for committee assignments.

II. Year Two—"Christ's Ministry in Our Community"

A. Some important changes

1. Deacons are added to the stewardship committee to be part of the planning process. The pastor should select representatives from the deacon board to serve with the stewardship committee.

2. The focus of Year Two is "Christ's Ministry in Our Community."

3. The Sundays of Launch Month have new themes and biblical texts.

B. Getting ready for Launch Month

1. Begin three to six months prior to Launch Month.

2. Incorporate additional church leaders in the planning process. This year the pastor, stewardship committee, and deacons will work together.

3. The pastor should select and appoint a chairperson for the stewardship committee. It is a good idea to appoint an assistant chairperson, with the intent that this person will become committee chairperson in Year Three.

4. Use the procedures outlined for Year One (pages 145-147). Select a new theme. (See example on page 158 and ideas on pages 169-170.) Do not leave out any steps, and don't do them the same way you did last year!

C. Launch Month

1. Start with a personal covenant to grow, and symbolize the covenant with Communion.

2. "Christ's Ministry in Our Community" is the primary focus during Year Two.

3. Challenge each member again to apply himself or herself to a month of study and growth in commitment to Christ. What will each member's ministry be in the community?

4. Remember that the "We Have This Ministry" presentation will highlight what your church is currently doing in community ministry. The "New Possibilities" presentation will look at new ministries your church could do in the community if members were to grow in their commitment to Christ. The "Hopes and Dreams" presentation will especially lift up the community ministries the church will do next year through the increased commitment of each member.

5. Make sure to include Prove-the-Tithe. Challenge members to grow beyond the 10 percent level. "To whom much is given; much more is required" (Luke 12:48, GNB).

6. Home visits of those who did not attend on Commitment Sunday are very important. We grow in commitment to Christ, or we fall away!

D. Following Commitment Sunday

1. Promptly send a thank-you letter confirming each person's renewed commitment.

2. Make certain that commitments of abilities, skills, and spiritual gifts are incorporated into the church's ministry as soon as possible.

3. Celebrate accomplishments and growth as biblical stewards.

E. The remainder of Year Two

1. Continue to have a monthly theme for growing stewards. Design your monthly themes to follow a pattern, such as the one illustrated on pages 169-170.

2. Apply each theme by using a specific weekly focus in Sunday school, in worship, in auxiliaries, at home, in school, at work, or in the community to encourage growth in biblical stewardship.

3. Remember to mail quarterly reports to each person who declared his or her intention. (Consider sending a reminder to anyone who declared a financial intention and after one month has given nothing.)

4. The committee needs to meet monthly to evaluate the progress of the entire ministry of "Call to Commitment." The committee members

should be reading books and reviewing video resources, filmstrips, and print materials. It is never too early to begin thinking about plans for Year Three.

III. Year Three—"Christ's Ministry Throughout the World"
  A. Some important changes
    1. The stewardship committee expands to include representatives from the mission board or society in the planning process. The pastor selects and appoints these persons.
    2. The focus of Year Three is "Christ's Ministry Throughout the World."
    3. A new theme is selected.
    4. The Sundays of Launch Month have new themes and biblical texts.
  B. Getting ready for Launch Month
    1. Begin planning three to six months before the start of Launch Month.
    2. Incorporate additional church leaders into the preparation process. This year the pastor, stewardship committee, deacons, and mission board or mission society will work together. The pastor should select and appoint the representatives.
    3. The pastor should also appoint a chairperson for the stewardship committee. If last year you had an assistant chairperson, that person may have developed enough to be chairperson.
    4. The pastor and committee should select a new theme for Launch Month. (See example on page 159 and ideas on pages 169-170.)
    5. Proceed with preparations as outlined in Year One (pages 145-147), but refrain from taking any shortcuts. They lead to "short" accomplishments. Also avoid doing any part exactly like last year.
  C. Launch Month
    1. Begin with a Communion service.
    2. Keep in mind, in all phases of the program, that the focus of Year Three is "Christ's Ministry Throughout the World."
    3. Encourage each member to covenant for a month of special study, growth, and commitment to Christ as each becomes aware of global ministry! This is the time to lift up overseas ministries and ways that your church is in partnership with our brothers and sisters on other continents.
    4. The presentations "We Have This Ministry," "New Possibilities," and "Hopes and Dreams" should address how growing commitment to Christ can enlarge our participation around the world.
    5. Proceed as in Year One, including Prove-the-Tithe. Remind members that the tithe is the "floor" and not the "ceiling." The counsel "as God has prospered you" may be the challenge to grow toward one-and-a-

half, two, or even two-and-a-half tithes! God is just as concerned about what stewards do with the 90 percent as the initial 10 percent!

6. The home visits of those persons missing Commitment Sunday are an important part of "making disciples." This is true of those making the visits as well as the persons being visited!

D. Following Commitment Sunday

1. Send a personal letter confirming each declaration of intention. (Be sure to use a different letter each year!)

2. Make use of all life commitments, such as skills, abilities, and spiritual gifts. This is a major responsibility! Nothing dampens enthusiasm as much as failure to use skills and abilities that have been offered!

3. Celebrate the growth of stewards. Have a church party including music, food, and a time of praise and thanksgiving as people share brief personal testimonies.

E. The remainder of Year Three

1. Be creative and persistent in this ministry of biblical stewardship for all ages, every month of the year.

2. The stewardship committee should meet monthly to work with the pastor to plan monthly events and experiences in stewardship development. Select topics and plan events to bring growth in ministry to the church, the community, and the global arena.

3. Remember to send the quarterly progress reports to each person who has made a commitment.

4. Continually evaluate program performance, looking for desired results. Plan next year's program, making necessary changes.

IV. Year Four—"Christ's Ministry in Our Church, Our Community, and the World"

A. An important change: The focus is now on all three dimensions of ministry. (See example on page 160.)

1. "Christ's Ministry Through Our Church"

2. "Christ's Ministry in Our Community"

3. "Christ's Ministry Throughout the World"

B. Launch Month

1. Because of the new people involved and the wider, three-fold focus, this could be the most exciting year yet! Use the process outlined in previous years, especially Year One (pages 145-147), but with new creativity and renewed vitality. (Avoid the trap of simply copying what has been done before.)

2. Some ideas to stimulate your thinking:

   a. Design special bulletin covers for each Sunday of Launch Month. Reflect different aspects of "Call to Commitment."

   b. Do a special newsletter on "The Christian As Steward." Have it include a special message from the pastor. Feature a page from children, a page from youth, and a page from adults. Extend the invitation to be responsible Christian stewards. Include a daily Bible study passage that fits your theme. (See the "Suggested Newsletter Article" on pages 170-171.)

   c. In the presentations to the Sunday school and in worship services, give the highlights of what the church is doing in ministry for those in the congregation, the community, the United States, and the rest of the world.

   d. For one of the Sundays in Launch Month, invite a missionary to speak.

   e. Have the Sunday school classes conduct a banner contest to portray the meaning of "Call to Commitment." Give appropriate recognition to all participating classes. Display all of the banners on Commitment Sunday.

   f. Involve your children and youth in as many ways as possible. They learn to become stewards by seeing and doing!

   g. Select four persons, one for each Sunday, who can share how "Call to Commitment" has enabled them to grow in their Christian life, including their tithe.

3. The emphasis must be on ministry and the potential for ministry in the local church, in the community, and in the world (including the United States). Challenge the congregation to its limits!

   a. In the church, ministry may be day care, senior citizen programs, singles ministry, marriage enrichment, or help for the hearing impaired.

   b. In the community, ministry may be serving the hungry and the homeless, combating alcohol and drug abuse, or recruiting and empowering volunteers to address the educational needs of the community.

   c. In the world, ministry may be adopting a special (over-and-above) overseas mission or a special ministry in the United States.

V. Year Five

Begin a new four-year cycle! The call to commitment, the call to discipleship, and the call to stewardship form a process that goes on *continuously!*

Call to Commitment
Program Suggestions

I. Personal Covenant to Study and Grow
(First Sunday)

Each person who attends worship on the first Sunday of Launch Month should make a commitment to be involved every Sunday for the next month! (A sample covenant can be found on pages 162-163. Prepare one that will suit the needs of your church and congregation.) Mail the covenant with a letter of invitation to every member urging attendance on the first Sunday. The pastor should prepare the letter with a special request for every person to be present for the Lord's Supper.

II. We Have This Ministry
(Second Sunday)

The idea here is to present the entire congregation with complete information about the ministry provided for the members of the church family. Stress the many different ways that the lives of people are touched. Let people share *briefly* from their personal experiences. Make presentations in the Sunday school as well as in worship. Presentations should be concise and to the point, with great enthusiasm. In addition, prepare an attractive handout specifically listing the various ministries of the pastor, staff, church leaders, boards, committees, auxiliaries, and others. "This is our ministry to the people who are part of this congregation." The pastor should write a cover letter to be mailed with this handout to every member. (If you desire, the chairperson of the stewardship committee can also sign the letter.) The letter and handout should be mailed the Monday *after* the first Sunday in Launch Month so that it will be received *before* the second Sunday.

III. New Possibilities
(Third Sunday)

This is an opportunity to excite people about additional ministries that are needed in the life of the church. The pastor and the stewardship committee should develop these "new possibilities," but the thoughts and ideas of other leaders in the church should be solicited and incorporated as appropriate. Whenever possible, portray these possibilities for ministry visually, even dramatically. Highlight ways that the lives of people can be blessed and enriched. Underscore that the church's ministry can be expanded and enhanced as each person grows in commitment to Christ. Make presentations in Sunday school groups as well as in the worship service. Prepare a descriptive and attractive handout. Ask a person in your congregation with graphic-arts abilities to prepare this piece. A letter of explanation and challenge should be written by the pastor and/or the committee chairperson. The letter and handout should be mailed the Monday *after* the second Sunday.

IV. Hopes and Dreams for the Year Ahead
(Fourth Sunday)

Plan achievable goals for the coming year. "Faith is the substance of things hoped for . . ." (Hebrews 11:1, KJV). Present clearly the vision for the next year in terms of specific ministries. Explain what each ministry will be like, to whom it will be addressed, and what human and financial resources will be needed to do it. Make presentations in Sunday school groups as well as in the worship service. Be sure these presentations are visual and not just verbal. Use slides, pictures, brief skits or pantomimes, and other creative methods. Develop a handout that is specific, concise, and appealing. Include the handout as part of the mailing sent out *prior* to Commitment Sunday (on the Monday *after* the third Sunday). This letter, written by the pastor, should speak of these hopes and dreams in the context of each person prayerfully examining his or her level of commitment to Christ. List the anticipated cost and people needs for each program you plan to implement. The letter can also be signed by the committee chairperson. For some samples of ways that hopes and dreams can be presented, see page 164.

V. Prove-the-Tithe Sunday

Ask every member for a commitment to tithe his or her income on the designated Sunday. Use a special envelope with a distinctive color. On each of the two Sundays preceding Prove-the-Tithe Sunday, have a person share what tithing means to him or her. Use a retiree, a married couple with children, or a single person living on his or her own. Distribute a leaflet or bulletin insert on tithing that can be taken home for further reflection. See "Stewardship Reflections" on page 165 for suggestions.

Prove-the-Tithe Sunday also can be used for some of the special days in the life of the church. It could be done on Women's Day, Men's Day, or other special days. Instead of suggesting a particular contribution, have every member bring his or her tithe. This would reinforce the vision of what the church could do in financial stewardship if all were committed to at least a tithe!

Whenever you use the Prove-the-Tithe ministry, be sure to celebrate both the growth and the potential for growth. Share the results with the congregation. It is essential to continually lift up the potential of the total church family.

VI. Alternatives to Prove-the-Tithe

If there are significant reasons why Prove-the-Tithe is not workable in your congregation, two other approaches can be considered to encourage growth in financial commitment.

A. The first is a survey of tithing potential. Prepare a bulletin insert using the example on page 166. Distribute the survey during morning worship. Make sure every person has a form and a pencil. Have each person circle his or her weekly income. If a person's income is below, above, or in between those listed on the insert, have that person write the amount in the box. Collect all of the forms and add up the total. This figure represents the total weekly income of those present in the congregation. Ten percent of that figure is the tithing potential of the church for each week. Multiply that number by fifty-two and you have the annual tithing potential for the church. It is important for the pastor to share these results with the church members and then stretch their minds with the ministry possibilities such potential represents. What is needed is commitment to Christ!

B. A simulated bank check is another approach for estimating tithing potential. Have each person complete a check on "God's Bank" for the amount of his or her tithe. Prepare a bulletin insert using the example on page 166. Use pastel paper similar to a bank check. Ask each person present at the worship service to fill in the date and write the dollar amount that represents 10 percent of his or her *weekly* income. Collect all of the "checks"; the total represents the weekly tithing potential of the church. Multiply by fifty-two. This gives you the annual tithing potential.

VII. Declaration of Intention

To encourage commitment of the total person to Jesus Christ, the commitment card, or faith-promise card, should invite each member to express more than a financial commitment. See the sample on page 167. It would help if people in the congregation knew in advance what spiritual gifts, skills, and abilities are needed most in the church's ministry. These could be printed in the Sunday bulletin on Commitment Sunday and/or outlined in the "Hopes and Dreams" handout. Be specific, such as the following: "We need twelve child-care volunteers who will serve two hours Sunday morning for a month, every other month." "We need two sound technicians for Sunday service." "We need four persons who have the gift of teaching junior high students."

VIII. Visiting Members Absent on Commitment Sunday

A. Prepare those who will do the in-home calling on those not attending worship on Commitment Sunday. Schedule this training for the Wednesday or Thursday evening just prior to Commitment Sunday. The deacons should be the core group; enlist enough others so that no one has more than four or five visits. Teach the callers to tell the church's story of ministry in a concise way with enthusiasm. Have the callers use the handouts that have been used during Launch Month ("We Have This Ministry," "New Possibilities," and "Hopes and Dreams"). It would help to use a different color for each handout. Help callers share their testimonies about the ministries that mean the most to them and about their growth as Christian stewards. Show them how to introduce the declaration of intention, and instruct them to allow some privacy as the person makes his or her commitment. Provide an envelope into which the person making a commitment can immediately put the declaration of intention.

B. Visitation should begin the afternoon of Commitment Sunday. Convene the callers at the church as early in the afternoon as possible. Or provide a basket lunch for them at the church right after worship. Review the nature and purpose of the visits. Make assignments and send the callers forth. Set specific times and dates when callers will report their results and turn in declarations of intention. They should complete all visits within two weeks. This may be harder for larger churches, but visitation offers real possibilities for growth in discipleship for those on the fringe of the church.

C. Prepare those persons who will be visited to receive the callers. This can be done in two ways. If you have a church newsletter, make it clearly known that members absent on Commitment Sunday will be visited and asked to make their declaration of intention. Everyone is being called to a renewed commitment to Christ. Second, the mailing on the Monday after the third Sunday should include a copy of the declaration of intention and should indicate that anyone not in attendance on Commitment Sunday will be visited. Ask them to welcome the visitors cordially. It is a good idea for the callers to set up appointments.

IX. Follow Through and Follow Up

A. A personal letter confirming each commitment and expressing appreciation from the church is a must! The pastor and the stewardship committee chairperson should both sign the letter.

B. Keep the congregation growing as stewards by including a paragraph about stewardship growth in every Sunday bulletin.

C. Use an offertory litany each week. Examples are on page 168. Write your own litany expressing your beliefs about prayer and biblical stewardship.

D. The pastor should share periodically about "Hopes and Dreams" as they begin to be fulfilled. Personal testimonies by people involved in the church's ministry, or by those who have benefited from that ministry, are excellent!

E. The stewardship committee, with the pastor, should select a monthly stewardship theme or focus. Some ideas are suggested on pages 169-170.

F. Send quarterly progress reports on financial giving to each person who made a commitment or declaration of intention.

G. Be intentional about including children and youth in all that is done to grow stewards. Use stories, visual aids, and words that persons of all ages can relate to and understand.

H. Distribute a leaflet on stewardship growth each month. We are what we think, and the more we think like stewards, the more we will grow as stewards.

I. The pastor, through the pulpit ministry and the worship service, must continually lift up biblical stewardship.

Example of Launch Month: Year One

Focus for the Year: "Christ's Ministry Through Our Church"
Theme for the Month: "Developing Healthy Christians"

Week	Theme and Text	Persons Responsible	Commitment Stressed	Program Elements
One	Mental Health "Let this mind be in you, which was also in Christ Jesus" (Philippians 2:5, KJV). (See also Romans 12:2; Ephesians 4:23.)	Pastor Stewardship Committee	Commitment starts with the mind.	Communion service Personal covenant to study and grow Sermon on text
Two	Physical Health "Present your bodies as a living sacrifice" (Romans 12:1, KJV). (See also 1 Corinthians 6:19, 20.)	Pastor Stewardship Committee	Commitment involves our physical being.	Presentation in Sunday school and worship: "We Have This Ministry" Prepare for Prove-the-Tithe Sermon on text
Three	Spiritual Health "Grow up in every way ... into Christ" (Ephesians 4:15, RSV). (See also Galatians 5:25; 2 Peter 3:18.)	Pastor Stewardship Committee	Commitment depends on spiritual development.	Presentation in Sunday school and worship: "New Possibilities" Continue preparation for Prove-the-Tithe Sermon on text
Four	Economic Health "To whom much is given ... will much be required" (Luke 12:48, RSV). (See also Luke 6:38; 2 Corinthians 9:6.)	Pastor Stewardship Committee	Commitment is revealed by what we share.	Presentation in Sunday school and worship: "Stewards Start with Tithing" Receive Prove-the-Tithe Sermon on text
Five (Optional)	Health of Our Souls "This night your soul is required of you" (Luke 12:20, RSV).	Pastor Stewardship Committee	Commitment without soul is not commitment.	Presentation in Sunday school and worship: "Hopes and Dreams" Receive declarations of intention Sermon on text Communion service Visits with nonattenders

Example of Launch Month: Year Two

Focus for the Year: "Christ's Ministry in the Community"
Theme for the Month: "The African American Family"

Week	Theme and Text	Persons Responsible	Commitment Stressed	Program Elements
One	Biblical Model for African American Manhood (Jeremiah 38:7-18)	Pastor Stewardship Committee Deacons	Unemployment of African American males and youth	Communion service Personal covenant to grow and study Prepare for Prove-the-Tithe Sermon on text
Two	Biblical Models for African American Womanhood (Genesis 16:3, 16:15; Numbers 12:1; Exodus 2:20, 4:20; 2 Kings 10:11-13)	Pastor Stewardship Committee Deacons	Teenage pregnancy	Presentation in Sunday school and worship: "We Have This Ministry" Prepare for Prove-the-Tithe Sermon on text
Three	Biblical Model for African American Youth (1 Samuel 18:22-23)	Pastor Stewardship Committee Deacons	Teenage drug addiction and alcoholism	Presentation in Sunday school and worship: "New Possibilities" Receive Prove-the-Tithe Sermon on text
Four	The African American Family (Genesis 10:6-12)	Pastor Stewardship Committee Deacons	The African American family: an endangered species	Presentation in Sunday school and worship: "Hopes and Dreams" Receive declarations of intention Sermon on text Visits with nonattenders

Example of Launch Month: Year Three

Focus for the Year: "Christ's Ministry Throughout the World"
Theme for the Month: "The Stewardship of People"

Week	Theme and Text	Persons Responsible	Commitment Stressed	Program Elements
One	Children "Let the little children come to me" (Mark 10:14, RSV). ". . . Except ye become as little children" (Matthew 18:3, KJV). (See also 1 Samuel 3:1; 2 Timothy 3:15.)	Pastor Stewardship Committee Deacons Mission Board	Ministry to children and ministry by children	Communion service Personal covenant to grow and study Involve children in worship service Describe ministries to children in the U.S.A. and overseas Sermon on text
Two	Youth "Be . . . an example of the believers" (1 Timothy 4:12, KJV). (See also Psalm 119:9; Luke 2:49; 1 Samuel 17:33, 37.)	Pastor Stewardship Committee Deacons Mission Board	Ministry to youth and ministry by youth	Use youth in service Presentation in Sunday school and worship: "We Have This Ministry" Describe ministries to youth in the U.S.A. and overseas Prepare for Prove-the-Tithe Sermon on text
Three	Adults "Bear one another's burdens" (Galatians 6:2, RSV). (See also Hebrews 6:10; 2 Thessalonians 1:3.)	Pastor Stewardship Committee Deacons Mission Board	Ministry to adults and ministry by adults	Use adults in service Presentation in Sunday school and worship: "New Possibilities" Describe ministries overseas and in the U.S.A. for adults, children, and youth Receive Prove-the-Tithe Sermon on text
Four	Persons of Special Needs "God's curse on anyone who deprives foreigners, orphans, and widows of their rights" (Deuteronomy 27:19, GNB). (See also Isaiah 1:17; James 1:27; Leviticus 19:14.)	Pastor Stewardship Committee Deacons Mission Board	Ministry to persons with special needs and ministry by persons with special needs	Use persons with special needs in service Presentation in Sunday school and worship: "Hopes and Dreams" Receive declarations of intention Sermon on text Visits with nonattenders

Example of Launch Month: Year Four

**Focus for the Year: "Christ's Ministry in Our Church,
Our Community, and the World"
Theme for the Month: "The Role of a Steward"**

Week	Theme and Text	Persons Responsible	Commitment Stressed	Program Elements
One	Ownership (Haggai 2:1-9)	Pastor Stewardship Committee Deacons Mission Board Christian Education Board	To serve persons in this church	Communion service Personal covenant to grow and study Presentation in Sunday school and worship: "Ministry in Our Church" Sermon on text Testimonies of members
Two	Responsibility (Mark 12:41-44)	Pastor Stewardship Committee Deacons Mission Board Christian Education Board	To serve persons in our community	Promote Prove-the-Tithe Presentation in Sunday school and worship: Testimonies on community ministries Sermon on text
Three	Trust (Genesis 22:3-14)	Pastor Stewardship Committee Deacons Mission Board Christian Education Board	To serve persons in all the world	Receive Prove-the-Tithe Presentation in Sunday school and worship: Invite a missionary Sermon on text
Four	Commitment (Job 13:15)	Pastor Stewardship Committee Deacons Mission Board Christian Education Board	To serve persons in church, community, and world	Presentation in Sunday school and worship: "Hopes and Dreams" Receive declarations of intention Sermon on text Visits with nonattenders

Resources

The following resources are included in this section. They can be used as is or adapted for your church. Photocopying for the following sections is permitted.

Sample Personal Covenant
Sample Presentation of Hopes and Dreams
Stewardship Reflections
Survey of Tithing Potential
Simulated Bank Check
Declaration of Intention
Offertory Litanies
Monthly Themes for Growing Stewards
Suggested Newsletter Article

Call to Commitment

A PROGRAM OF PERSONAL AND CHURCH RENEWAL

Sample Personal Covenant

"Call to Commitment" Covenant

In response to Jesus' call to commitment and ministry, I covenant with God and the members of our church

— to engage in a four-week period of reexamination and renewal, seeking to be open to God's leading for my own life and ministry and that of our church.

— to be present for worship each of the next four Sundays of our "Call to Commitment" emphasis.

— to participate in special group experiences during the church school hour for the next four Sundays.

— to search the Scriptures and my own heart and life through daily Bible reading and reflection during "Call to Commitment" month.

— to reexamine my abilities, interests, concerns, and opportunities in order to understand more fully my calling as a Christian and the ministry God wants me to perform as a follower of Jesus Christ.

— to consider possible forward steps in personal growth and in Christian witness and service in every area and relationship of life.

— to consider and share with church leaders possible ways of improving and expanding our church's ministries and outreach.

— to consider prayerfully my stewardship—my grateful response to God's generosity and my responsible management and use of *all* that God has given me: life, new life in Christ, time, abilities, money, and relationships.

_____

(Please sign and keep as a reminder.)

A Personal Covenant with God and My Church

A Self-Examination of
My Commitment to Christ As Lord

As I come to this service of Communion and am reminded again of God's forgiving, saving love revealed in Christ and his cross, I realize the debt of love I owe. "Love so amazing, so divine, demands my soul, my life, my all."[1]

Remembering that Communion is a time of self-examination (1 Corinthians 11:28), I want to consider my life and review and renew my commitment to Christ as Lord.

When I accepted Christ as my Savior, I recognized his sacrificial gift of life to me and committed my life to him, to follow him and to join with him in the work of his kingdom.

When I joined Christ's church, I promised to be a faithful member, upholding it by my prayers, my attendance, my service, and my gifts.

How Well Have I Followed Through on These Commitments?

1. What am I doing to increase my understanding of the Christian faith and my effectiveness as a servant of Christ?

2. How often and how seriously do I study the Scriptures in an effort to better understand God's will for my life?

3. Am I a better informed, more knowledgeable Christian now than I was when I accepted Christ? than I was last year? last month? last week?

4. How much time do I spend in prayer and meditation other than at mealtime or in public worship?

5. Am I using my God-given abilities in the service of Christ and others?

6. Am I giving a worthy proportion of my financial resources for the work of Christ?

7. Am I a vital, involved member of a study or service group within the church?

8. Am I growing in expressing Christian love for people both within and outside of the fellowship of our church?

[1]"When I Survey the Wondrous Cross," Isaac Watts, 1707.

How Am I Doing?
Where Do I Need to Grow in My Commitment to Christ?

As I look back over this list of self-examination questions, I know that there are several things I need to do, forward steps I need to take, to more fully implement my commitment to Christ as Lord of my life.

What I need to do:

_____

_____

_____

_____

_____

_____

_____

_____

_____

_____

_____

_____

_____

_____

Sample Presentations of Hopes and Dreams

Ministry to Families

1. Hold two weekend conferences on parenting skills. Have one for all parents. Hold a second conference just for single parents. Begin on Friday evening, perhaps with a covered-dish meal. Have skill sessions on Saturday morning and Saturday afternoon. Provide a light lunch. Bring it to a climax in Sunday school and Sunday worship with a focus on parenting today.
Cost—$300 per conference
People needs—child care, meal servers, parenting consultants

2. Sponsor quarterly family-recreation days. Families need encouragement and guidance in learning to play together. Hold on Saturdays or certain holidays. A day might include a train ride, a bus tour, a visit to a museum or historical site, a hike, or a day in the park.
Cost—$150 per event (transportation, fees, food)
People needs—volunteers to coordinate the events

3. Help families understand the realities of aging and the changes that are experienced. Hold conferences on
   Aging parents
   Empty nest
   Illness/death of a spouse or child
   Midlife years
   Health-care aspects of aging
   Living in retirement
   Adult children in crisis
Cost—$100 per seminar
People needs—coordinators and seminar leaders

Development of Christian Disciples

1. Conduct new-member training for all who join the church.
2. Develop sponsors for each new member during his or her first year.
3. Hold Saturday "kids clubs" for social, personal, and spiritual development.
4. Conduct youth jamborees several times a year.
5. Hold adult personal-enrichment seminars.
6. Sponsor an annual marriage-enrichment experience.
7. Sponsor or cosponsor a career-enrichment seminar and/or a vocational conference that includes church vocations.
8. Provide health-enrichment seminars.

Stewardship Reflections

The Stewardship of Business

"Did you not know that I must be about My Father's business?" (Luke 2:49, NKJV).

Jesus never lost the keen sense of the stewardship of his "business." This was evident during his public ministry on many occasions; he often declared things such as "I must work the works of him that sent me" (John 9:4, KJV) or "I came . . . not to do mine own will, but the will of him that sent me" (John 6:38, KJV).

Jesus regarded his lifework as a trust to be used wisely for God. The example of Christ leaves his followers with no other alternative. Faithful Christians will be good stewards of their ability to do God's work.

The Christian church has the privilege and responsibility to call every follower of Christ to recognize that one's ability to work is a stewardship that each one must administer wisely and well. You belong to Christ not only on Sunday but also throughout the week! Every type of work, no matter how humble, can become a sacred privilege depending on the reverence with which the Christian approaches it. Your duty to God is not fully met by prayers, fasting, and tithing. The stewardship summons demands your possessions, time, talents—your very life!

Dare to Be a "Moneychanger"!

Recorded in Matthew 21:12, Jesus' act of driving the moneychangers from the temple is usually seen as criticism of those who were using the temple for commercial purposes. Yet, there is a very positive lesson in this Scripture. Think for a moment. When a person brings money to be used in "God's house" *to further God's program and purposes,* the money is changed into life!

Dare to be a "moneychanger"! Our money can be changed into food for the hungry, college tuition for a young person, the gospel for a godless nation, or medicine for an indigent person. By its right use, money can talk in many languages and aid in bringing men and women to a wonderful relationship with Christ Jesus.

It is our responsibility as Christ's stewards not to let money change us. God has given us the power, knowledge, and means by which to change money. Let's begin today to be "moneychangers for Christ"!

Selfishness

To ignore the obligation that inherited blessings and privileges have brought to us is the height of sinful selfishness! The Christian who does nothing to pass the gospel on to others is guilty of unfaithfulness as a steward of the manifold grace of God, is robbing both God and other people, and is unworthy of the name Christian.

How do *you* plead?

Survey of Tithing Potential

Purpose

To discover the potential amount available for Christian ministry if all were to tithe by faith.

Total Weekly Income

Circle your *weekly income*. If your income is below, above, or in between the figures listed, write the figure in the box below.

100	110	120	130	150	160	170	180	190	200	210
220	275	300	325	350	375	400	425	450	475	500
550	600	650	700	750	800	850	900	950	1000	1050	1100

If your weekly income does not appear above, write the amount in the box:

Simulated Bank Check

$$\$$$

_____ , 19 _____

Pay to the order of _____ $ _____
(your church's name)

God's Eternal Bank
Heaven and Earth

Memo: _____ My Weekly Tithe _____   _____ I Am Christ's Disciple _____

$$\$$$

Declaration of Intention

Recognizing my need to grow as a steward, I commit myself as follows to helping our church achieve our ministry goals for the year ahead:

I will help by committing in faith

_____ hours each week in service to the church's ministries
_____ my spiritual gift of _____
_____ my skill or ability of _____

As a further expression of my renewed dedication to Jesus Christ, I will also commit my financial resources to the lordship of Christ and to the ministries of our church as follows:

As God prospers me, I will dedicate in faith _____ percent of my income to the Lord. Therefore, it is my intention to support Christ's ministry in our church by sharing $_____ per week/month (circle one) in the coming year.

Signature _____

Offertory Litanies

LEADER: Every person shall give as able, according to the blessing of the Lord.

CONGREGATION: **We give unto the Lord the glory due his name, bringing an offering as we come into his courts.**

LEADER: Be very thankful in all things. The opportunity to give is in itself a blessing to those who are obedient.

CONGREGATION: **We offer ourselves and all that we are to thee, grateful for thy love and mercy.**

UNISON PRAYER: **God, as your children, we turn to thee with a renewed commitment and a deeper sense of thanks for all thy blessings. Amen!**

LEADER: As we give the tithe of substance to the Lord, let us do so with a generous and unselfish motive.

CONGREGATION: **Let us exercise this gift of the Holy Spirit as we worship the Lord with our generosity.**

LEADER: Giving is a spiritual gift to be exercised by all believers.

UNISON: **Let us exercise this gift of the Holy Spirit as we worship the Lord through giving the tithe.**

LEADER: The One who supplies seed to the sower will supply and multiply your resources.

CONGREGATION: **Thanks be to God for his inexpressible gift!**

LEADER: Under the test of this service, you will glorify God by your obedience and by your generosity.

UNISON: **We will be enriched in every way, hence we joyfully bring our tithes and offerings to the storehouse.**

LEADER: According to the blessings of the Lord our God, we bring our tithes and offerings willfully.

CONGREGATION: **We consecrate ourselves to you, Lord.**

LEADER: It is required of stewards that they be found trustworthy.

UNISON: **We consecrate ourselves and all you have given us to you, Lord Most High.**

UNISON PRAYER: **For as much as our strength is in thee, mercifully grant that thy Holy Spirit may in all things direct and rule our hearts; through Jesus Christ our Lord. Amen.**

LEADER: Every one to whom much is given, of that person will much be required.

CONGREGATION: **And to the person to whom others commit much, they will demand the more.**

LEADER: Let no one boast!

CONGREGATION: **For the world, life, death, the present, and the future are all ours, and we are Christ's, and Christ is God's.**

Monthly Themes for Growing Stewards

1. Stewardship of People
   - Children—ministry to children, ministry by children
   - Youth—ministry to youth, ministry by youth
   - Adults—ministry to adults, ministry by adults
   - Persons of special need—ministry to persons of special need, ministry by persons of special need

2. Stewardship of Peace
   - Inner peace
   - Home and family
   - Community and nation (world peace)

3. Stewardship of Planning
   - Church and church groups
   - Personal and family
   - Wider Christian fellowship
   - Neighborhood and community

4. Stewardship of Life
   - Food for the hungry
   - Freedom for the oppressed
   - Shelter for the homeless
   - Dignity and worth for the poor

5. Stewardship of the Gospel
   - As communicator (witness to family and loved ones)
   - As model and teacher (witness to friends and associates)
   - As partner and advocate (witness to community, state, nation)
   - As provider and sustainer (witness to the peoples of the globe)

6. Stewardship of Justice
   - Racial
   - Religious
   - Human rights
   - Economic

7. Stewardship of Self
   - Intelligence
   - Feelings
   - Spiritual gifts
   - Skills and abilities
   - Value system

8. Stewardship of faith
   - Congregational worship

- Personal
- Learner or teacher in Sunday Christian education
- Modeling faith in work, school, home

9. Stewardship of Resources
   - Time
   - Money
   - Estate (insurance, will, and so forth)
   - Possessions (cars, house, furniture, jewelry, and so forth)

10. Stewardship of Relationships
    - Family
    - Work or school
    - Church
    - Community

11. Stewardship of Earth
    - Environment (water, air)
    - Plants and animals
    - Food, clothing, shelter
    - Minerals

12. Stewardship of Health
    - Physical
    - Mental
    - Spiritual
    - Economic

Suggested Newsletter Article

Stewardship is the foundation for a better, more complete relationship with God. The word *stewardship* comes from the word *oikonomia*. A steward (*oikonomos*) was known during the period 323 B.C. to 30 B.C. as a householder, tenant, treasurer, accountant, manager, or trustee. The English translation, *stigweard,* is made up of two medieval roots: *stig* (house or household) and *weard* (keeper).

Any research into the subject of stewardship would clearly show that a steward does not own or hold rights of possession to those things entrusted to his or her care. We can find numerous biblical examples. Look at Matthew 25:14-30, Luke 12:37-48, and 2 Corinthians 5:10. A study of these passages shows us that God is the maker, and God remains the owner of all created things—past, present, and future. Genesis 1:1 states, "In the beginning God created the heavens and the earth" (RSV). That ownership also includes our lives, for we, too, are created beings.

We have only to look to Jesus, our master teacher in matters of faith, to see a perfect example of stewardship. Jesus lived his life with total dedication, with a driving sense of purpose and responsibility to God. While still a boy, he expressed in the temple a strong awareness of purpose and responsibility: "Did you not know that I must be about My Father's business?" (Luke 2:49, NKJV). This statement shows an accountability to God. That is stewardship. At God's request, Jesus died on the cross at Calvary for our salvation. This is his final act as a faithful steward. Jesus never ceased to recognize his responsibility to God.

Jesus' life is the model of stewardship. It leads Christians to determine how they use and care for their *bodies,* what they do with their *money,* how they develop and use their *talents,* and how and where they spend their *time.*

Each steward will one day be called before God to account for the management of all responsibilities received from God. It will not simply be a matter of how productive a steward has been, but rather how faithful the steward has been in using the opportunities given by God.

Notes

Foreword

1. Frances Ridley Havergal, "Take My Life, and Let It Be," 1874.

Preaching Stewardship: The Word of God

1. W. E. Burghardt, *The Soul of Black Folk* (Chicago: Johnson Reprint Corporation, 1903), 190.

2. William A. Henry III, "God and Money Part 9," *Time,* 22 July 1991, 28.

3. Werner Hans Bartsch, ed., *Kerygma and Myth* (New York: Harper Torchbooks, 1961), 47.

4. Claude H. Thompson, *Theology and Kerygma* (Englewood Cliffs: Prentice Hall, Inc., 1962), 142.

5. Ibid.

6. James S. Stewart, *Heralds of God* (New York: Charles Scribner's Sons, 1964), 78.

7. John Huxtable, *The Bible Says* (Richmond: John Knox Press, 1962), 113.

8. Ibid., 110.

9. Thompson, 75.

10. Ibid., 109.

11. Huxtable, 109.

12. Bartsch, 41.

13. Ibid.

14. Carter G. Woodson, *The Mis-Education of the Negro* (Trenton: African World Press, 1990), 65.

15. Ibid., 66.

16. Thompson, 143.

17. *Holy Koran,* Surah III, Section 10, note 419.

18. J. Massyngberde Ford, "Revelation," *The Anchor Bible,* Vol. 38 (Garden City, New York: Doubleday & Co., Inc., 1975), 90.

19. Thompson, 26.

20. Ibid.

21. Ibid., 14.

22. Ibid., 23.

23. Ibid., 47.

24. Ibid., 129.

Where Your Treasure Is

1. Raymond Rasberry, "Only What You Do for Christ Will Last," 1963. Copyright Raymond Rasberry. All rights reserved. Used by permission.

In Need of a Miracle

1. "Ain't Got Time to Die," traditional.

172

Kids for the Kingdom

1. William Barclay, *The Gospel of Mark* (Philadelphia: Westminster Press, 1975), 242.

2. Joy Duckett Cain, "Parenting: The Spiritual Connection," *Essence*, December 1991, 96.

3. Sari Howitz, "For Area Black Students, Project Excellence Can Spell College," *The Washington Post,* 13 May 1992.

4. *The Virginian-Pilot and Ledger Star,* 2 May 1992.

5. C. Eric Lincoln and Laurence H. Mamiya, *The Black Church in the African Experience* (Durham: Duke University Press, 1990), 309.

6. Jawanza Kunjufu, *Motivating and Preparing Black Youth to Work* (Chicago: African American Images, 1986), 41.

7. Ibid.

8. Tom Sine, "Shifting the Church into the Future Tense," *The American Baptist*, 19 March 1992, 32.

9. Harriett E. Buell, "A Child of the King," 1877.

Some Time for the Mind

1. Floyd Massey, Jr., and Samuel Berry McKinney, *Church Administration in the Black Perspective* (Valley Forge: Judson Press, 1976), 49.

2. Eliza A. Hewitt, "More About Jesus," 1887.

Such As I Have

1. John Naisbitt and Patricia Aburdene, *Megatrends 2000* (New York: William Morrow & Co., Publishers, 1990), 270.

2. Douglas John Hall, *The Steward: A Biblical Symbol Come of Age* (New York: Friendship Press, 1982), 88, quoting Robert L. Heilbroner, *The Great Ascent.*

3. Ibid., 92.

4. Harry Emerson Fosdick, *The Meaning of Service* (New York: Garden City Books, 1950), 18.

5. Ibid., 65.

6. E. F. Schumacher, *Small Is Beautiful: Economics As If People Mattered* (New York: Harper and Row, Publishers, 1975), 168.

AIDS and the Stewardship of Aid

1. "Grim report on spread of AIDS virus," *Philadelphia Inquirer,* 4 June 1992.

2. Ibid.

3. *Ebony,* April 1992, 105.

4. Angela Mitchell, "AIDS: We Are Not Immune," *Emerge,* November 1990, 30-44.

5. Earl E. Shelp and Peter Mansell, *AIDS: Personal Stories in Pastoral Perspective* (New York: The Pilgrim Press, 1987), 2.

6. C. Everett Koop, "Acquired Immune Deficiency Syndrome," U.S. Healthcare Healthy Outlook Program (Pamphlet), 8.

7. Ervin "Magic" Johnson has authored a book on AIDS, *What You Can Do to Avoid AIDS* (New York: Time Books).

8. Wallace E. Fisher, *A New Climate for Stewardship* (Nashville: Abingdon Press, 1976), 42.

9. Ibid., 44.

10. Ibid.

11. Waldo J. Werning, *The Stewardship Call* (St. Louis: Concordia Publishing House, 1970), 18.

12. A growing number of helpful resources is available, including Neal Hitchens, *Fifty Things You Can Do about AIDS* (Los Angeles: Lowell House, 1991) and James McKeever, *The AIDS Plague* (Medford, Oreg.: Omega Publications, 1986).

13. Adelaide A. Pollard, "Have Thine Own Way," 1907.

Assessing Historical Financial Patterns of the African American Church

1. Gloria Naylor, *Linden Hills* (New York: Ticknor and Fields, 1985), 155.

2. Carter G. Woodson, *The History of the Negro Church* (Washington, D.C.: Associated Pubs., Inc., 1921, 1990), 257.

3. Julius Lester, *Do Lord Remember Me* (New York: Holt, Rinehart and Winston, 1984), 176-177.

4. Woodson, ix-x.

A Thriving Church

1. Robert Lemon, *God's People and Church Government* (Tulsa: Harrison House, 1983).

2. Knofel Staton, *God's Plan for Church Leadership* (Cincinnati: Standard Publishing Co., 1982).

3. Warren Wiersbe, *Be Wise* (Wheaton, Ill.: Victor Books, 1983).

4. J. Alfred Smith, Sr., *Giving to a Giving God* (Washington, D.C.: Progressive National Baptist Press, 1992), 6.

Selected Bibliography

Print Resources

Bassler, Jouette M. *God and Mammon: Asking for Money in the New Testament.* Nashville: Abingdon Press, 1991.

Cunningham, Richard B. *Creative Stewardship.* Nashville: Abingdon Press, 1979.

Discover Your Gifts. (A workbook.) Grand Rapids: Christian Home Reformed Missions.

Hall, Douglas J. *The Steward: A Biblical Symbol Come of Age.* Rev. ed. New York: Friendship Press, 1990.

Johnson, Douglas W. *The Tithe: Challenge or Legalism?* Nashville: Abingdon Press, 1984.

Roberts, Robert H. *Encouraging the Tithe.* (A tithing-emphasis program.) Valley Forge: World Mission Support, 1993.

Schumacher, E. F. *Small Is Beautiful: Economics As If People Mattered.* New York: Harper and Row, 1975.

Smith, J. Alfred, Sr. *Giving to a Giving God.* Washington, D.C.: Progressive National Baptist Press, 1992.

Vallet, Ronald E. *Stepping Stones of the Steward.* Grand Rapids: William B. Eerdmans Publishing Co., 1989.

Van Benschoten, A. Q., Jr. *What the Bible Says About Stewardship.* Valley Forge: Judson Press, 1983.

Walker, Wyatt Tee. *Common Thieves.* New York: Martin Luther King Fellow Press, 1986.

Video Resources

How Do I Respond? (Thirteen-minute video cassette.)

James Forbes. *Preaching Christian Stewardship.* (Three video cassettes, two fifty-minute presentations per cassette.)

The Names of Money. (Thirteen-minute video cassette.)

Did You Ever See a Steward? (Seven-minute video cassette, for children ages five to nine.)

For additional resources on stewardship, contact your denominational offices.

Also Published by Judson Press

Additional Stewardship Resources

What the Bible Says About Stewardship, A.Q. Van Benschoten, Jr. 0-8170-0993-0

Money, Motivation, and Mission in the Small Church, Anthony Pappas. 0-8170-1146-3

Sermon Resources

Afrocentric Sermons: The Beauty of Blackness in the Bible, Kenneth L. Waters, Sr. 0-8170-1199-4 (Available December 1993.)

Best Black Sermons, William M. Philpot, editor. 0-8170-0533-1

Contemporary Biblical Interpretation for Preaching, Ronald J. Allen. 0-8170-1002-5

Cups of Light and Other Illustrations for Sermons and Meditations, Clarence W. Cranford. 0-8170-1142-0

From Mess to Miracle and Other Sermons, William D. Watley. 0-8170-1154-4

"How Shall They Hear?": Effective Preaching for Vital Faith, Samuel D. Proctor. 0-8170-1172-2

Outstanding Black Sermons, J. Alfred Smith, Sr., editor. 0-8170-0664-8

Outstanding Black Sermons, Vol. 2, Walter B. Hoard, editor. 0-8170-0832-2

Outstanding Black Sermons, Vol. 3, Milton E. Owens, Jr., editor. 0-8170-0973-6

Preaching in Two Voices: Sermons on the Women in Jesus' Life, William D. Watley, Suzan D. Johnson Cook. 0-8170-1173-0

Sermons from the Black Pulpit, Samuel D. Proctor, William D. Watley. 0-8170-1034-3

Sermons on Special Days: Preaching Through the Year in the Black Church, William D. Watley. 0-8170-1089-0

Those Preachin' Women: Sermons by Black Women Preachers, Ella Pearson Mitchell, editor. 0-8170-1073-4

Those Preaching Women, Vol. 2: More Sermons by Black Women Preachers, Ella Pearson Mitchell, editor. 0-8170-1131-5

What Makes You So Strong? Sermons of Joy and Strength from Jeremiah A. Wright, Jr., Jini Kilgore Ross, editor. 0-8170-1169-2 (Available November 1993.)

Women: To Preach or Not to Preach? 21 Outstanding Black Preachers Say Yes! Ella Pearson Mitchell, editor. 0-8170-1169-2

African American Church Resources

All God's Chillun Got Soul, Morrie Turner. 0-8170-0892-6

Church Administration in the Black Perspective, Floyd Massey, Jr., Samuel B. McKinney. 0-8170-0710-5

The Church in the Life of the Black Family, Wallace C. Smith. 0-8170-1040-8

God's Transforming Spirit: Black Church Renewal, Preston R. Washington. 0-8170-1129-3

In Goode Faith: My Story by W. Wilson Goode, W. Wilson Goode, Joann Stevens. 0-8170-1186-2

Interpreting God's Word in Black Preaching, Warren H. Stewart, Sr. 0-8170-1021-1

The Ministry of Music in the Black Church, J. Wendell Mapson, Jr. 0-8170-1057-2

Paul's Message of Freedom; What Does It Mean to the Black Church?, Amos Jones, Jr. 0-8170-0840-3

Poems of a Son, Prayers of a Father, Matthew L. Watley, William D. Watley. 0-8170-1183-8

Roots of Resistance: The Nonviolent Ethic of Martin Luther King, Jr., William D. Watley. 0-8170-1092-0

Samuel Proctor: My Moral Odyssey, Samuel D. Proctor. 0-8170-1151-X

"Somebody's Calling My Name," Wyatt Tee Walker. 0-8170-0980-9

Telling the Story: Evangelism in Black Churches, James O. Stallings. 0-8170-1124-2

Pastor's Resources

Activating Leadership in the Small Church, Steve Burt. 0-8170-1099-8

Caring for the Small Church: Insights from Women in Ministry, Nancy T. Foltz. 0-8170-1175-7 (Available December 1993.)

Christian Education in the Small Church, Donald L. Griggs, Judy McKay Walther. 0-8170-1103-X

Church Office Handbook for Ministers, Betty Powers, E. Jane Mall. 0-8170-1011-4

Dedication Services for Every Occasion, Manfred Holck, Jr., compiler. 0-8170-1033-5

Developing Your Small Church's Potential, Carl S. Dudley, Douglas A. Walrath. 0-8170-1120-X

Litanies for All Occasions, Garth House. 0-8170-1144-7

Living in the Image of Christ, Hans-Ruedi Weber. 0-8170-1106-4

Lord, Make Us One: Understanding Personalities in the Church, John W. Sloat. 0-8170-1101-3

A Manual of Worship, New Edition, John E. Skoglund, Nancy E. Hall. 0-8170-1184-6

The Minister's Handbook, Orlando L. Tibbetts. 0-8170-1088-2

Mission: The Small Church Reaches Out, Anthony Pappas, Scott Planting. 0-8170-1174-9 (Available August 1993.)

The Pastor in a Teaching Church, David M. Evans. 0-8170-0970-1

Prayers for All Occasions: For Pastors and Lay Leaders, Roy Pearson. 0-8170-1127-7

Prayers From Adoration to Zeal, C. Welton Gaddy. 0-8170-1190-0

Premarital Counseling Handbook for Ministers, Theodore K. Pitt. 0-8170-1071-8

The Salvation and Nurture of the Child of God, G. Temp Sparkman. 0-8170-0985-X

The Star Book for Ministers, Edward T. Hiscox. 0-8170-0167-0

Available from your local bookstore or Judson Press.